OLD GARDEN FLOWERS

OLD GARDEN FLOWERS

— Brian Halliwell —

BISHOPSGATE PRESS

Acknowledgement

Colour illustrations by kind permission of
Sutton Seeds Ltd. Torquay.

British Library Cataloguing in Publication Data

Halliwell, Brian
  Old garden flowers.
  1. Plants, Ornamental 2. Flower gardening
  —History
  I. Title
  635.9′09   SB404.5

  ISBN 0-900873-80-9

All enquiries and requests relevant to this title should be sent to the publisher,
Bishopsgate Press Ltd., 37 Union Street, London, SE1 1SE

Printed by Whitstable Litho Ltd., Whitstable, Kent

CONTENTS

INTRODUCTION

Gardening took its place as a leisure pursuit for the gentry during the 16th century and for the next 300 years was to remain the prerogative of the wealthy. Whilst cottagers had gardens, these were for growing plants for food, flavouring and medicine; space was too valuable for non-utilitarian plants no matter how beautiful.

During the 19th century, England was to change from an agrarian society to the most industrialised nation in Europe. The industrial revolution saw the movement of people from rural areas into towns and cities which had to expand rapidly to accommodate them. This century was to see changes in the English class structure. Manufacturers who made fortunes in trade were the nouveau-riche who in emulating the established gentry, built imposing mansions set in spacious gardens outside expanding conurbations. Managers of industry and men of the professions became the new middle class who were to create suburbia on the outskirts with villas and semi-detached residences each with its moderate sized garden. Within towns for the working class, were built tenements, cottage-type dwellings and terraces of small houses with communal or private gardens. Gardening was now a pastime available to all.

There have always been fashions in plants; in some, e.g. auricula, although popularity has waxed and waned, they are as popular now as they were 400 years ago; others though have remained in favour for much shorter periods: decades or for just a few years. The media today has made us all fashion conscious so in striving for novelty in our gardens, plants beloved by parents and grandparents are out of favour and difficult to find. It is perhaps, to counter this loss of what are now considered as old-fashioned plants that the cottage garden movement is gaining in strength. A cottage garden is not literally an area around a small rural dwelling but refers to a garden style in which there is an absence of formality with an indiscriminate arrangement of plants of all kinds.

Here with cultural details are plants of every kind that can be used in specimen planting, shrubberies, topiary, hedges, herbaceous border, bedding and rock and herb gardens. In earlier centuries any plant grown in a garden had to be primarily of use to man, if it had beautiful flowers, this was of secondary importance. Even with the surge of interest in growing herbs, readers may be surprised at the uses made of plants which are now grown solely for ornament. The multiplicity of common names may make readers realise that botanical names are not a sign of affectation but that this universal language has a use even by an ordinary gardener.

In my choice, I have avoided specialist plants for which there are societies to foster cultivation and I have concentrated on those which in my opinion are unjustly neglected.

Asian Ranunculus

It is curious that the English, with their aversion to foreign names have never found any other name for *Ranunculus asiaticus*. Most species of *Ranunculus*, whether native or alien, have been called 'buttercup', sometimes 'crowfoot', but this plant has remained 'Asian ranunculus' even though it extends into two other continents. It may have been brought into England by returning crusaders, but it is generally considered to have come from gardens of the Turkish court in the middle of the sixteenth century, along with the tulip; both have a great diversity of flower form with a similar colour range. In a very short space of time, tulips had become so widely grown that they were the most fashionable of all spring flowering bulbs of the seventeenth century; a popularity which they have continued to hold to the present day. Asian ranunculus was not to reach a position of eminence until the eighteenth century, and by the end of that century it was already falling from fashion, never to regain its status, and today they are rare in English gardens.

Ranunculus asiaticus has a wide distribution, extending through the western regions of Iran, Iraq and Syria into Israel, and is to be found in both Asiatic and European Turkey as well as on some of the islands in the Mediterranean (Cyprus, Crete and Rhodes), and also in many of the countries of North Africa. The plant consists of a number of small tubers somewhat larger than a rice grain which are summer dormant; they come into growth with the arrival of the autumn rains, flowering in winter or early spring and with the seeds ripe and scattered by the onset of summer.

One kind at least was being grown by Gerard in his garden at Holborn in 1596, although in the 1633 revision of his *Herbal* seven kinds are mentioned, some single, others double, and there is an illustration showing one flower growing out of another. Most, if not all gardeners of the seventeenth century were growing Asian ranunculus in any number of colours, both single and double, although it was the latter which were most favoured. Some of the colours were white, yellow, pink, mauve, red and purple so deep as to be almost black; there were self-colours, bicolours and flowers striped, spotted or edged. Although large numbers of seedlings were raised, only a small percentage proved to be double. In the hope of obtaining new colours, especially of doubles, large quantities of tubers were imported into England. Many gardening writers were complaining about the large number of tubers that were dead on arrival, and about poor colours and scarcity of doubles among the survivors. In the eighteenth century Asian ranunculus became the most fashionable of the spring flowers, challenging, if not overtaking, the tulip. To supply an ever-increasing demand there were nurseries specialising in just this one plant. James Maddocks, who had a nursery in Walworth near London, was offering several hundred different kinds from the many thousands of seedlings which he was raising annually. New forms and colours were sought from amongst the seedlings and these were then propagated vegetatively. At this time, there were two groups of doubles; the turban and the peony-flowered, while they were also listed under the countries from which they were imported or bred: African, Persian, Turkish, Dutch and Scotch.

During the seventeenth and eighteenth centuries a florist was not a person who made a living from selling cut flowers, but someone, usually an amateur, who specialised in growing many sorts of a single or a few kinds of plants. Florists formed themselves into clubs and displayed their plants in competition at floral feasts. By the end of the seventeenth century at least three cities were holding floral feasts: Norwich, London and York, during the eighteenth century they were held in almost every town and city throughout the United Kingdom. During these two centuries the main florist's flowers were: auricula, tulip, anemone, hyacinth, polyanthus, Asian ranunculus, carnation and pink. Although these feasts were probably originally organised for and by the gentry, artisans were allowed to compete and were soon carrying off the prizes. A floral feast would be held at a local inn and the charge for entrance included a lunch before the flowers were inspected. Competition in the cultivation of these plants was very keen in every strata of society, and many books were written on cultivation and the qualities expected of a prize winning flower. By the early nineteenth century, the floral feast had been replaced by the competitive flower show that we know today, in which a very wide range of garden and glasshouse produce was displayed.

By 1820 the leading Asian ranunculus nurseryman could offer only 400 different kinds, about half the number offered by James Maddocks 30 years earlier. In 1826, Henry Phillips in *Flora Historica* is bemoaning the decline of the Asian ranunculus and by 1871, William Sutherland in *Handbook of Hardy Herbaceous and Alpine Flowers* says, . . . 'ancient florists used to boast that *Ranunculus asiaticus* was more numerous in varieties than all other flowers; they are not so now, and the trade in named sorts is trifling'. It is surprising that when bedding became a garden fashion, Asian ranunculus did not return to favour for spring display. The decline has continued during the twentieth century, and in the few bulb catalogues which still offer them only mixtures seem to be available. The single forms are occasionally grown by rock garden enthusiasts in alpine houses, and they do sometimes appear in alpine shows. It seems curious that a plant once so fashionable has fallen so completely out of favour. Even though they can be damaged by winter cold, polythene tunnels ought to be satisfactory for extensive cultivation as a cut flower. In New Zealand and the southern states of Australia, the Asian ranunculus is the most widely grown of all spring flowering 'bulbous' plants. There they are usually treated as annuals being raised from seed, for breeding has produced strains which come true to colour and are fully double.

If a gardener is to introduce these plants into his garden by means of tubers, these should first be planted into boxes containing a mixture of sand and peat, and watered carefully until growth begins. In an area with mild winters, planting out can be done in autumn; but where the winters are cold, do not start the tubers into growth until the coldest weather has passed. When tubers are to be kept under protection; a temperature just above freezing is all that is necessary, and only enough water should be given to keep the plants and their leaves alive. A few seedsmen are offering this plant, and there are now colour strains of singles and doubles available which breed more or less true. Seed should be sown in boxes of a soil or peat based compost in gentle heat in early spring, or larger quantities can be sown *in situ* under a cold frame. Keep the seedlings growing until they have made strong plants, after which water can be withheld until they die down; begin to water again in autumn or winter, just before planting out.

Balsam

This plant has had a number of similar common names over the centuries all with the same root as that used in the present day: 'balsamina', 'balsamine', 'female balsam' and 'balsam apple'. Until 1753, its botanical name was *Balsamina foemina,* the female balsam, occasionally female balsam apple, whilst *Balsamina mas* was the male balsam, which today we know botanically as *Mormordica balsamina* and commonly as balsam apple despite the fact that it belongs to the cucumber family. The use of the same common name for plants from two different families came about because of the similarity in shape of the two fruits at a time when it was not necessarily floral characteristics which were used to classify plants. In

Species Plantarum Linnaeus was to use the name of *Impatiens balsamina;* perhaps it was his sense of humour which made him choose *Impatiens* for this genus of plants which was so impatient that the slightest touch on their ripening fruit would cause them to explode and forcibly eject the seeds. Gerard in his *Herbal* had made this comment about the balsam: 'its fruits are apples rough and hairy when they be ripe, which cleaves them asunder of themselves and cast abroad their seed'.

Balsam was already known in Germany by 1542, for Leonart Fuchs, professor of botany at Tübingen, writing in his *Herbal* was to call it 'a recent introduction, planted already in many gardens'. It is interesting to speculate how *Impatiens balsamina,* a native of India, China and Malaya had come into Europe from such distant lands so early! Although there is a mention of balsamine by William Turner in *Names of Herbes* published in 1548, it seems to apply to *Mormordica balsamina.* There is no doubt though that Gerard was growing it in his garden at Holborn in 1596, and there is an illustration in his *Herbal* of 1597 with a description: 'floures of incarnate colours tending to blewnesse having small spurs or tails annexed thereunto as hath the Larkesheele (Larkspur) of faire light crimson colour'. He continues: 'These plants do prosper best in hot regions; they are strangers in England and doe with great labour and industry grow in these cold lands'. Most of the gardeners in subsequent centuries make similar observations, although Philip Miller did in part demur, for he wrote of singles in his *Gardener's Dictionary:* 'These sorts are so hardy as to rise in the full ground; and where seeds are scattered will come up in the following spring!' although he, like other gardeners, considered the doubles less than easy to grow, commenting that it was difficult in most years to collect ripe seed.

In the seventeenth and eighteenth centuries, seed was sown on hot beds and when the seedlings were large enough, they were transplanted onto a second newly prepared bed, from where they were carefully lifted when large enough for transplanting. A hot bed consisted of a pile of fresh manure covered by a layer of soil; the fermenting manure generated heat which warmed the soil. Plants may have gone directly into the garden, although they were often put into containers and brought to the flowering stage first. All books recommend copious watering in the summer, and several comment that in hot summers their flowers remained fresh whilst those of many other plants wilted or shrivelled.

The first plants grown in England were single and had mauve or purplish pink flowers, although one with white flowers was being grown in about 1620 by John Goodyer. In *The Solitary Gardener* of 1706, which was a translation into English of a work by two Frenchmen, Liger and Gentil, all balsam flowers were described as red. In 1768 Miller at the Chelsea Physic Garden was growing red, white and striped flowers, both singles and doubles; he had received seed of the doubles from the East Indies. The

Reverend William Hanbury in 1771 had red, white, purple and variegated flowers, both single and double, of which he said: 'Some are very large and double of all sorts and some variegated with scarlet and white and white and purple and these large sorts among gardeners have the name of Immortal Eagle Flower'. By 1826, in *Flora Historica* Henry Phillips was saying that 'The love of novelty even in plants often leads us from the old established favourites to less interesting objects; and when fashion points the way, we as naturally follow as if this supreme directress were incapable of error. We shall therefore entreat the gay nymph to renew her smiles at this eastern plant . . . We have frequently observed the balsam in the gardens of Paris having more the appearance of a brilliant flowering shrub than an annual plant ornamenting the quarters of the Royal gardens of the Tuilleries and the Luxembourg by its petals of scarlet, crimson, brick red, purple white variegated, part coloured or delicate blush'. From a journal called *Horticultural Transactions*, Phillips quotes a Mr. Fairweather who speaks of plants which are four feet in height and fifteen feet in circumference, with strong thick stems furnished from side branches from bottom to top which are covered with large double flowers.

The nineteenth century saw the development of the new garden fashion of bedding, and balsam came to be used in summer to fill beds in Victorian parterres. It was also being used for summer decoration of conservatories. To cater for the demand, seed houses were carrying out breeding programmes to supply the demand for novelty, with an extended colour range: many more shades of pink, almost pure blue, violet and cream, with the emphasis on doubles. There were two main groups of doubles, camellia and rose-flowered, each of which had two varieties a taller one which was two feet (600mm) high, and a shorter one 12in. (300mm) high.

Although balsams remained popular well into the twentieth century, they began to lose favour after the Second World War and are little grown today. So many once popular bedding plants seem to have disappeared, and one can understand why this has happened with balsam when one thinks of English summers, which can be so cold and dull. This plant has had peaks and troughs of popularity over the last 400 years, and may once again rise in favour as the whims of fashion change.

Seed should be sown in a glasshouse in early spring in gentle heat. Prick out the seedlings as soon as they are big enough to handle, putting them singly into small pots of a soil- or peat-based compost, and as the pot fills with roots, transfer them to one larger. Plant into the position in which they are to flower when the danger of frost has passed. When balsam is to be flowered in a container, make sure that it ends up in one at least 6in. (150mm) in diameter and when this has filled with roots apply a weekly dressing of a weak liquid feed.

Bergamot

'Bergamot' today is a common name used for two different plants, *Monarda fistulosa* and *M. didyma*. The original bergamot was a kind of orange from whose skin an oil was extracted. Bergamot takes its name from the town of Bergamo in northern Italy, where this orange was widely grown to produce the oil which has been used in perfumery since the seventeenth century. There also is a bergamot mint, an alternative name for lemon or Eau-de-Cologne mint. The use of the name 'bergamot' for these different kinds of plant is due to a similarity in the fragrance of the leaves.

The introduction of *M. fistulosa* into England is attributed to John Tradescant on his first visit to Virginia in 1637. It is recorded in the list of plants growing in his garden at Lambeth in 1656 but it had been included in John Parkinson's *Theatrum Botanicum* of 1640 as *Origanum fistulosum canadense*. The appendage of *canadense* must raise doubts as to it being a Tradescant introduction for it seems unlikely that John Tradescant ever visited Canada. In the seventeenth century all garden plants had to be useful as well as beautiful: *M. fistulosa* was used as a strewing herb for sweetening the atmosphere of parlours and bedrooms (a seventeenth-century deodorant). This species is common right across Canada, and extends southwards as far as Mexico. In the United States the plant is called 'wild bergamot', a name by which it used to be known in England.

John Bartram, a Pennsylvania farmer with a consuming interest in plants, discovered *M. didyma*. Although self-taught, he has been called the first American botanist. He made many trips into the little-explored countryside of the north-eastern United States and south-east Canada in his search for plants, and it was on a trip which began in 1743 that he discovered *M. didyma* on the shores of Lake Ontario. The seed which he collected was sent to his friend and patron Peter Collinson in London, who flowered a plant in 1746. This species, which extends southwards from New York State to Tennessee is called Oswego Tea after a small town in New York State where an infusion of the leaves was used as a herbal remedy. It was known by this name in England for more than a century, and is even known by it occasionally today. It was to become 'scarlet' or 'crimson bergamot' whilst in more recent times the colour adjective has been dropped. Another occasional name used in the United States and in England is 'bee balm'. Its fresh leaves are sometimes used for flavouring hock, moselle and punch as well as sponge cakes, and the dried leaves can be a constituent of pot-pourri.

The genus commemorates Nicholas Monardes (1493–1588), a physician and botanist of Seville, who had written a book about America translated into English as *Joyfull Newes out of the newe found world*. The specific epithet of *fistulosa* refers to the plant's hollow stems whilst *didyma*, meaning 'a pair', indicates the two long and prominent stamens.

Although *M. fistulosa* was the earlier of the two species to be introduced into this country, it is infrequently seen in gardens today. It is more suitable to a dry soil and tends to lack vigour, although it can reach 5ft (1.6m); the flowers which are really lilac or mauve pink are sometimes described as being purple. *M. didyma* is more common, with larger, more spectacular flowers on neater and shorter growth. As it seems to prefer a moister soil than the other species, it performs better in English gardens. There are a number of named cvs of varying heights with flowers of red or pink; the colour range has been extended by hybridising with *M. fistulosa* to provide mauves and purples.

These are excellent plants for the herbaceous border or island beds, and can be used to bring summer colour into the herb garden. Flowering declines with age and plants should be lifted every three years at the end of winter, pulled apart, retaining the stronger shoots from the perimeter of the clumps, for replanting into a well cultivated soil containing plenty of organic matter.

Bleeding Heart

Bleeding heart has been applied to a number of species of the genus *Dicentra* but it is usually intended for *D. spectabilis*. Other common names reserved for this plant which are perhaps more descriptive, even amusing, are: dutchman's breeches, chinaman's breeches, our-lady-in-a-boat, lady's locket and lyre-flower. The generic name is derived from the Greek and refers to the two spurs on the flower, while the specific epithet means 'showy'. An early botanical name occasionally found even today in some books was *Dielytra spectabilis*, which seems likely to have been a spelling mistake made by Linnaeus who had never seen a living specimen of the plant.

Although it was introduced into England in the first decade of the nineteenth century, the plant did not establish itself then, and was to be reintroduced by Robert Fortune in 1846. Robert Fortune was born in Berwickshire and had trained at the Royal Botanic Gardens, Edinburgh. Like many other Scots, he came south to seek his fortune and became an employee of the Horticultural Society (later to become the Royal Horticultural Society) at their gardens at Chiswick. Dr John Lindley, who at that time was assistant secretary to the Horticultural Society, chose Fortune to make a trip to China, which had just become accessible to Europeans. He was to see the plant in flower when he visited the island of Chusan in 1844, growing in the garden of a mandarin. When he asked its name, he found that the translation of it was 'red and white moutan flower' ('Moutan' came to be more usually associated with tree peonies, where it was said to mean 'greatest' or 'king' of flowers). On its arrival in England, *D. spectabilis* was grown in the Society's gardens under glass until its hardiness was proved. Even today it has a reputation for tenderness. Precocious growth can be damaged by late spring frosts so severely that plants are seriously weakened and in cold wet winters even killed, but it can tolerate much lower temperatures if kept dry. It was to become extremely popular in the gardens of the wealthy, and in middle-class suburbia.

Shirley Hibbert, the editor of *Floral World and Gardener's Magazine*, was to say that, though cheap and common, it was a very charming flower of cottage gardens. In *Hardy Herbaceous and Alpine Flowers* of 1871, William Sutherland says that it 'is so familiar to all lovers of flowers that a description of it would be superfluous. It will be enough to be reminded that it is not surpassed in brilliancy and grace by any known hardy perennial plant and it is withal most easy to cultivate'. It found favour with William Robinson, but one is less assured of its estimation in Reginald Farrer's eyes when we read in *The English Rock Garden*. 'And every gardener knows the most bleeding of all hearts, the towering and regal *Dicentra spectabilis* of spring so much more rudely, if aptly styled when liberal gardeners give the grosser name of Dutchman's breeches'.

Following its introduction into England, it must have arrived soon afterwards in the United States, for by 1851 it was so commonly available in nurseries that it was retailing at 25 cents. It was being grown for sale in nurseries along the eastern seaboard where winters are extreme, so its hardiness would seem to be proven. Although winter temperatures in the east can fall very low, the ground would be covered with snow which would protect the roots, keeping them dry, so that by the time the snow had gone, sharp spring frosts would be unlikely. In English gardens today *D. formosa*, which is native to the Pacific seaboard, is the most common species. This seems to have been unknown in eastern North America as a garden plant in 1851, and yet it is said to have been growing in English gardens as early as 1810.

Dicentra spectabilis was to remain popular in English gardens right up to the Second World War, but by the 1960s it had become uncommon. Its arching stems with their large pendant locket-like flowers make it an attractive plant for the front of a herbaceous border or island bed, and in addition to the showy flowers there are attractive grey-green leaves which remain on the plant well into the summer. Whilst the usual flower colour is two shades of pink, there is also a variety which has pure white blooms.

Once planted, it is better not to dusturb *D. spectabilis,* and during the replanting of borders every third year, to dig round the plants rather than lifting and dividing. In an ordinary soil although it may begin flowering when it is about 9in. (225mm) high, in late spring, by the time the flower stem is fully developed it may reach 2ft (600mm). At this height the stem is strong enough to support the flowers, but in a rich soil a longer and weaker stem develops which will benefit from the support of brushwood which will allow the stem to arch gracefully. Propagation is not easy unless one has a warm glasshouse. Cuttings of young shoots, taken as the new growth develops in the spring, with a portion of root still attached and inserted in a mixture of peat and sand in a warm propagating case, can be induced to root.

Borage

The generic name in *Borago officinalis* was used as a common name in England in the Middle Ages, but this came to be anglicised to 'borage' spelt in various ways. 'Borago' or 'borage' is derived from a Latin word *burra* which was a coarse cloth or a garment made from it; perhaps a comparison of the rough texture of the cloth with the bristly leaves of the plant. This annual of eastern Europe has been so long cultivated that it has become naturalised in countries far outside its natural range. As long ago as the first century AD, Pliny was recommending an infusion of the leaves in wine to make men merry and joyful. Culpepper considered borage to be a British plant, saying that it was common around London and mentioning Deptford and Rotherhithe. It is, however, not native, having arrived in England at the time of the Norman conquest, even though a Roman introduction is equally probable. As early as the thirteenth century it is recorded as growing in English gardens: there is mention of it by John Gardiner in his book *Feate of Gardening* of 1440; it is in Fromond's list of herbs, dating from about 1500, and it appears in *Libellus* of 1538 by William Turner, as 'bugloss'. Beginning with John Gerard in 1597, and in many books of the seventeenth century, it becomes possible to read about the uses for borage: juice extracted from the leaves, and made into a syrup with sugar or honey, expelled sadness and melancholy, comforted the heart, clarified the blood, was an antidote to poisonous bites and stings, cured yellow jaundice, was used to bathe tired, reddened and sore eyes, easing the discomfort of the itch, and removed spots, pimples, freckles and the marks of ring worm. A borage tea was given to young ladies and the lovelorn to cure swooning and unrequited love. In the kitchen it was used as a pot herb: chopped leaves were added to pottage (a thick broth) before serving. Seedling leaves were used as ingredients in a salad which was made more colourful and therefore more appetising by adornment with fresh flowers in summer, and flowers pickled in wine vinegar in winter. Fresh flowers were floated in claret, stirrup, fruit cup and punch. Finely chopped young leaves added to wine and beer in summer produced a cooling effect. Borage is an ingredient of the modern day 'Pimms'.

An obvious place for growing borage is the herb or vegetable garden when it is to be used in medicine or for cooking. As it has large and colourful flowers it can be allowed into the flower garden as a constituent of annual borders or as a summer filler for herbaceous borders, island beds and shrubberies. Blue, the least common colour for flowers in general, is the most usual one for borage, 400 years ago, however, white flowers were common, and in 1771 the Reverend William Hanbury mentions a borage with red flowers and another with variegated leaves.

As borage has a short flowering season, about 3 weeks, there should be a succession of sowings at two week intervals throughout spring and early summer so that there is a continuity of young leaves and flowers. Seed sown in early spring will take perhaps eight weeks to flower, but later sowings, as it becomes warmer, will result in flowers in less than four. From the earliest of the spring sowings it will be summer before the first blooms appear, but the season can be brought forward by making autumn sowings which will overwinter as young plants. Choose a weed-free piece of ground in full sunlight that is not too rich; fork over, tread to firm, apply a light dressing of lime and rake to produce a smooth surface. Sow the seed into shallow drills about 12in. (300mm) apart and thin the resulting seedlings to the same spacing. Seed is fairly freely set in most summers but it can be sparse if the weather is cool or dull. It should always be collected for future use, although once plants have become established self-sown seedlings will always appear. William Hanbury wrote more than 200 years ago that a few plants would flower and scatter seeds which would come up in such abundance that they would be difficult to control. Even so birds are very fond of borage seed and may well strip the plant before the gardener can gather it for his own requirements. At certain seasons birds also seem to be attracted by the flowers which they can tear to pieces.

'Box' is the anglicisation of the generic name in *Buxus sempervirens;* the specific epithet means 'everliving'. *Buxus sempervirens* extends from the western seaboard of Europe through countries on either side of the Mediterranean and into western Asia. It is a woody plant which can vary from a dwarf, many-stemmed shrub to a tree with a trunk up to 30ft (10m) high. There are young angled stems which have opposite, entire margined leaves, oval or oblong in shape and up to an inch (25mm) in length and half an inch (12mm) in width; clusters of tiny yellow single sex flowers develop in the axils of the leaves on the previous season's growth during spring. Following pollination and fertilisation, trilocular capsules develop which contain black shining seeds.

Box was known to all the western ancient civilisations and was brought into England by the Romans; traces of box branches have been found in the middens of Silchester. Although box is and has been common in a few localities in England, notably Box Hill in Surrey, it is probably not a native tree. Because its timber has always been valued, it may be that the Romans had made plantations in England during their occupation, and that it was from these that box escaped and has spread and naturalised a few localities on chalk soil. The wood, which is so heavy that it sinks in water, is hard, white and close grained and has had many uses. In his *Sylva* of 1664, John Evelyn says, 'it do furnish the Inlayer and Cabinet Maker with pieces, rare undiluted and full of variety. Also of box are made wheels, or Shrivers as our Ships Carpenters call them and pins for Block and Pulleys; pegs for Musical Instruments; Nut Crackers; Weavers Shuttles, Hollar Sticks, Bump Sticks and Dressers for the Shoe Maker; rolling pins, Pestles, Mall Balls, Beetles, Tops, Tables, Chessmen, Screws male and female; bobbins for bone-lace, spoons, nay the stoutest Axle Trees but above all:'

Box Combs bear no parts
In the militia of the Female Art
They tie the Links which hold our Gallants fast
and Spread the Nets to which fond lover hast.

The wood was also used until the present century to make wooden blocks for printing and engraving. Evelyn also advocated the oil of box as a cure for venereal disease and for toothache, whilst herbalists used it to cure leprosy, falling sickness and to staunch bleeding. An infusion of leaves was also used as a hair dye. Throughout Europe, box seems to have had connections with funerals. The way from the house of death to the church was strewn with box, whilst mourners carried sprigs with them to be cast onto the coffin before the grave was filled; it was common practice too to plant box on graves. At Candlemas, holly used in Christmas decorations in the home was taken down and replaced by box, which remained there until Easter eve. On the Sunday before Easter, box was often used as a substitute for palm leaves to decorate the church and branches were use to fill home fireplaces at Whitsuntide.

Box has always found a place in gardens. The Romans planted bushes in their villa gardens in Italy and the other countries which they occupied, and cut them into bizarre shapes. When topiary reappeared in the gardens of Europe in the sixteenth century, it began a fashion which has continued until the present day, although it reached a peak of popularity in Holland and Germany and to a lesser extent in England during the seventeenth century. It was in sixteenth-century England that gardening began to be practised as an art; first in the form of knots, intricately patterned tiny beds which were to develop into the elaborate geometrical and symmetrical designs of the parterres of the seventeenth century. These beds were edged at first with wood, stone or slate, but these materials came to be replaced by living plants, which, though they included lavender, lavender cotton and rosemary, was more often box. This was clipped at frequent intervals to keep lines sharp, tops low and level and to form coloured edgings to the beds. Also part of these elaborate patterns would be statues or urns as well as pillars, pyramids, cubes and spheres of clipped box.

It must have been sometime during the sixteenth century that dwarf box was introduced into England from Holland, for throughout the next two centuries it was to be called Dutch box. When the naturalised landscape gardens of the eighteenth century swept away the formality of the previous century, box retreated to the vegetable garden to be used for edging paths and beds. In the nineteenth century formality returned to some extent with the advent of bedding. A Victorian parterre developed, but this was simpler than that of two centuries earlier and had larger beds, some of which were edged with box. At this period evergreen shrubs, including box, came to be used around the garden and were trimmed regularly to keep them neat and tidy. When the shrub border made its appearance at the beginning of the twentieth century evergreen shrubs were planted to provide interest during the winter when the deciduous subjects were naked. It is therefore relatively recently that so many of the named cvs of box have become known. Some of these were reintroductions from earlier times, but others were selections from sports which had occurred on box in cultivation. There is now a whole range of cvs varying from the dwarf, which is known as *suffruticosa*, to the arborescent; some are upright, others are pendulous, whilst there are leaves of varying shapes and sizes with colours ranging through the many shades of green to yellow, and others banded or patterned with yellow or white. Box grows naturally on chalk, but it is tolerant of a wide range of soils and although it will not grow on a badly drained soil, it will tolerate one which is thin and dry. When box is to occupy a piece of ground for a long time it should be thoroughly prepared to ensure that the sub-soil is broken up and that copious quantities of organic matter are included.

Today box is mostly used to produce hedges, although it is a suitable plant for the topiary enthusiast who has only a small garden; he should select a strong growing cv such as *longifolia*. Dwarf box can be used for edging paths or beds and as ground cover when it is closely planted on steep banks. There has been an increasing interest in the restoration of seventeenth-century gardens, in which there would be an extensive use of box in parterres. Some of the upright forms and those which are naturally domed can be used in a shrub border, whilst the prostrate and less vigorous pendulous forms can be planted in the larger rock garden. The arborescent forms and the more vigorous pendulous cvs can be used for specimen trees on lawns. Many of the smaller cvs of *B. sempervirens* are suitable for training into bonsai subjects.

In hedges, edging and topiary it is necessary to keep the plant trim and tidy, which necessitates clipping. One trim a year is all that is necessary if this is carried out in summer after the new growth is complete. Whilst hand clipping is preferable, for extensive plantings of box electrical trimmers will be used, but the cutting blades must be very sharp and regularly cleaned otherwise they tear branches producing a very untidy appearance which remains obvious for at least a year.

All the varieties referred to above should be propagated by cuttings which are taken of new growth at the end of the summer and can continue throughout autumn and into early winter. In areas with mild winters cuttings can be rooted in the open ground, but better results will be obtained in frames, polythene tunnels or glasshouses. This same treatment can be used for dwarf box, especially when large numbers of plants are required, but they will not reach planting size for about three years. When larger plants are required in small numbers immediately, the old plants can be lifted at the end of the winter just before new growth is about to commence, and pulled apart into two pieces, each of which is replanted. Large quantities of dwarf box are difficult to obtain in this country.

Buttercup

The first gardens in England were made by the Romans in the central courtyards of their villas. When the power of the Romans waned and many returned to Rome, their villas fell into ruins and their gardens disappeared, so that gardening became no more than an adjunct of agriculture, to produce food. Some plants survived in the gardens of monasteries, which were then the centres of healing. The Normans were more concerned with defending themselves and suppressing the barbarians in a conquered country than to indulge in gardening. Throughout some 400 years of troubled times, the homes of the most important landowners were castles or fortified manors where there was no space for gardens. It was only with the advent of more settled times that the gentry replaced their decaying castles with new houses which were large with spacious rooms lit by large windows and with elaborate furnishings. The house became a status symbol and ostentation spread to the surrounds of the house, so the first garden styles came into being. The dawn of the seventeenth century saw gardening become established when it became a leisure pursuit for the gentry along with hunting, shooting and fishing. To cater for the new interest, nurseries sprang up and the first books on gardens were written. Because gardens now had to impress, it was plants that had come from overseas which were considered more desirable, whereas in earlier centuries, the earliest plants to be brought into gardens were mainly those from the countryside. Obviously those with the brightest and largest flowers would be the first to come into cultivation. All the time a watch would be kept for anything that differed from the usual type in size, habit of growth, leaf shape, size and pattern and flowers that were larger or of different colour or form. During the sixteenth century, double flowers became fashionable and remained so throughout the next two centuries; this brings us to the subject of this section: the buttercup.

Many of the 14 or 15 kinds of British buttercup have produced double flowers, but probably only three of these are still around today: the meadow, bulbous and creeping respectively, with the Latin names *Ranunculus acris*, *R. bulbosus* and *R. repens*. The first of these as *R. acris* 'Flora-pleno' is still commonly offered for sale by nurseries specialising in herbaceous plants, as it makes a useful plant for the herbaceous border or for island beds. From a loose rosette of deeply cut jagged leaves arise stems of up to 3ft (1m) with early summer flowers ¾in (18mm) in diameter which are fully double. Gerard claims to have been the first person to have found this plant: 'it chanced that walking in the field next to the (Globe) theatre by London in the company of a worshipfull merchant named Mr Nicholas Lete found this one kinde there with double flowers which before that time I had not seen'.

Gerard also records the double form of the bulbous buttercup which he says 'Mr Thomas Hesketh found growing wilde in the towne fields of a small village called Hesketh not farre from Latham (Lytham St. Annes) in Lancashire'. There is an illustration showing a hen-and-chickens form of the bulbous buttercup where one double flower grows out of another. Although it has the common name of bulbous buttercup the rootstock is more turnip-like, and from the usual rosette of buttercup-like leaves a flower stem of about 12in (300mm) develops with often only an early summer single flower. Today many plants offered as *R. bulbosus* 'Pleniflorus' are incorrectly named.

Although neither Gerard nor Parkinson seem to have known the double creeping buttercup, it was being grown at the John Tradescants' garden at Lambeth in 1656. This double form increases in the same way as the single, by sending out stems along the ground with a new plant developing at the end. Whilst it can be planted at the front of a herbaceous border or island bed, it needs watching for it can become invasive.

Many of the double kinds of British buttercups came to be called 'bachelors buttons'. These 'buttons' consisted of tiny pieces of cloth which were placed one on top of the other and held together by a stitch; they could be fixed easily onto clothes by unmarried men who lived in bothies.

Butterfly Flower

Buddleia davidii commemorates two men of the church: one English, the other French. Linnaeus named the genus after the Reverend Adam Buddle, rector of Great Franbridge in Essex in the early eighteenth century; Buddle was an amateur botanist with considerable knowledge of mosses and grasses. The specific epithet commemorates the Abbé Armand David, a missionary priest who was resident in China from 1862 to 1876. His arrival in China followed the opening up of that country to the peoples of the West. While he was there, he was able to follow up his great interest in studying all aspects of natural history, making three trips into the interior of the then little explored country. On these expeditions he made extensive collections of plants, animals, birds, fishes, reptiles and insects, which he sent back to the Museum of Natural History in Paris. Among the plants he collected were some that were new to science; the best known of those named after him are: the dove tree, *Davidia involucrata, Clematis armandii* and *Buddleia davidii.* There is also an animal which bears his name, Père David's Deer, and he may have been the first European to see the giant panda. It was among the herbarium specimens sent back to Paris in 1869 that Franchet recognised a previously unrecorded *Buddleia* which he was to name in memory of Armand David. The first living plant of this species was brought back to England by Dr Augustine Henry in about 1887. Dr Henry was a medical doctor trained in Dublin who became an officer in the Imperial Maritime Customs Service of the Chinese government, and then turned his energies to plant collecting. The *Buddleia* which he had found came to Kew where William Hemsley, unaware that it had already been named by Franchet, called it *B. variabilis.* Although this is a very variable plant and such an epithet seemed apt, cynics have suggested that he used *variabilis* because of the many different ways he had seen *Buddleia* spelt. (It was from a later collection of about 1901, made by E. H. Wilson for the firm of Veitch, that the coloured forms of this plant have been developed).

Buddleia davidii is widespread in the mountains of northern China in the provinces of Hupeh, Ichiang and Szechuan. It forms a medium to large shrub, up to 10ft (3m) high, although on occasions it can grow into a small tree twice this height. Its young stems are square in cross section, with opposite lance-shaped leaves of varying lengths: there are cvs with variegated leaves. From mid to late summer, there are tapering conical bunches of flowers which vary from pure white to lilac (the commonest colour) through to mauvish red and bluish purple. The flowers are fragrant and attract butterflies which feed on the nectar. So numerous are these insects that 'butterfly bush' or 'shrub' has become a common name, more appealing than the rather clumsy Americanism, 'buddlebush'. During a warm autumn, seed capsules will ripen and disseminate the fine chaffy seed, and seedlings can pop up in many places in the garden. During and after the Second World War, the ruins of bombed London were screened by butterfly bushes which had grown from seeds either caught up amongst the rubble or lodged in cracks and crevices of the broken-down buildings.

It is an easy shrub to grow in gardens, and seems to be indiscriminate in its choice of soil; although it grows satisfactorily in the poorest soil, it performs best when the soil is good. Plant at the end of the winter among other shrubs, either bare rooted or from a container. Do give it plenty of space, for it is a vigorous grower and can grow to over 6ft (2m) in a year. When established it benefits from hard pruning which improves the size of the flower spike; on an unpruned bush, flowers may not be more than 4in. (100mm) in length, but if hard pruned they can exceed 12in. (300mm).

Pruning should be carried out during the winter when the plant is dormant; cut back all shoots almost to ground level or close to a previously trained framework. Following pruning, apply a dressing of general fertiliser at the rate of 2 ounces per square yard (68 grams per square metre) over the root run. As mentioned above, self sown seedlings can appear in gardens and these should be rigorously rogued and only those with the finest flower colours allowed to remain.

Named cvs are propagated by cuttings. If there is a frame or glasshouse, take the cuttings in late summer and insert into a very sandy compost. For those gardeners who have no such structures, hardwood cuttings can be prepared which may be rooted in the open ground. From the prunings of new growth cut the stems into pieces about 10in. (250mm) in length and insert them into a slit trench so that only about 2in. (50mm) protrudes.

Canary Creeper

There is much uncertainty about canary creeper: its botanical name, the derivation of its common names and how it arrived in England. It can be found under any of three botanical names: *Tropaeolum aduncum,* in which *aduncum* means a hook – a reference to the spur on the back of the flower; *T. canariensis,* suggesting the country of origin, the Canary Islands; and *T. peregrinum,* where the specific epithet means immigrant. In addition to 'canary creeper', there is 'canary vine', 'fringed canary flower', 'canary bird flower' and 'fringed yellow Indian cress'. As the Spanish name for the plant is *paxarito,* which means 'a little bird', 'canary' in many of the names suggests an avian connection rather than a reference to the islands. 'Indian cress' had been the common name of the first species of tropaeolum, *T. minus,* introduced into English gardens in the sixteenth century, because the taste of the leaves resembled those of water cress, so 'fringed yellow Indian cress' is an apt description. The 'canary creeper' is a native of Chile and Peru; the first Europeans to see it were the Spanish conquerors of South America in the sixteenth century. On their return home, Spanish soldiers took seed with them leaving some behind in the Spanish Canary Islands to be grown in gardens. The climate suited this plant and it was able to escape from cultivation so that when European botanists visited the islands two centuries later, the canary creeper seemed to be growing wild. This part of its history may well have been the reason why Linnaeus classified the plant with the specific epithet of *peregrinum,* for he gave Peru as its country of origin.

Its documented arrival into Europe was in the early years of the eighteenth century, and is attributed to Louis Feuillée. Father Louis Feuillée, a member of the Order of Minims, had a wide range of interests:

astronomy, hydrology, cartography and botany. It was while he was exploring the coastal regions of Chile and Peru to prepare maps and charts of towns and ports that he discovered canary creeper in the Cuzco region of southern Chile, growing on forest fringes of the middle slopes of the Andes; seed was sent back to Le Jardin des Plantes in 1709. It seems to have been slow in establishing itself in gardens, for if Linnaeus had seen a living plant when he described it in *Species Plantarum,* it must have been in Sweden some 20 years before it appeared in England; a Mr Benjamin Bewick is credited with introducing it to England in 1775. Although it was firmly in cultivation in England by 1809, when a 'canary creeper' flower from a Mr Vere's garden was used by an artist as a model for an illustration in the *Botanical Magazine,* the first mention of it in a book is by Jane Loudon in *The Ladies' Flower Garden* of 1840

By the end of the nineteenth century it was being widely grown in gardens as a half-hardy climber and also in conservatories for summer display. This fast growing summer climber with pretty flowers has always been overshadowed by the other more spectacular species of *Tropaeolum.*

Although it is so often regarded as an annual, it is in fact perennial and will reappear every spring in gardens where winters are mild. It is a strong grower and needs plenty of space for development, for it can make up to 10ft (3m) of growth in one growing season. Avoid planting or sowing in a rich soil otherwise growth can be excessive, foliage rank and flowering sparse. It is an accommodating plant, for it seems indifferent to the type of soil and will grow in sun or shade. In the first few weeks following germination it keeps to a single stem before it begins to produce side-shoots. Leaves, which are alternate, and greyish or blue-grey in colour, are lobed, resembling the fingers of a hand; its stems are supported by the leaf stalks curling around their support, which in a garden can be a trellis, vertical or parallel wires or a wigwam of cut branches or canes. Sow seed where plants are to flower, in a rather poor soil in mid-spring; blooms will appear in mid to late summer and continue well into the autumn. Seeds sown in containers in a warm glasshouse will provide young plants which can be out planted into the garden as soon as the danger of frost has passed to provide earlier flowering.

Candytuft

Today 'candytuft' is always written in the singular form, yet in the seventeenth century when it was a newcomer to English gardens, it appeared in the plural as 'candy tufts' or 'tufts of Candie'. 'Tufts' indicates the tufted habit of the plant, and 'Candy' or 'Candia' is the old name for Crete. Gerard records that he received seed from Lord Edward Zouche, who had collected it on Candy in the last quarter of the sixteenth century. Its botanical name is *Iberis umbellata,* indicating that the Iberian Peninsula is the home for many species of this genus, and in fact Parkinson, in *'Paradisus in Sole'* of 1629 used Spanish tufts as an alternative name for candytuft. Although in writing about this plant Gerard had also called it 'mustard of Candie' and 'Candie Thlaspi', there are no virtues given for it either by him or by any other herbalists of the seventeenth century. A common name that was in use during the eighteenth century however, was 'sciatica weed' so it must have been used as a cure, or at least a treatment, for this ailment.

Although it has long been favoured by country folk for their cottage gardens it has been shunned by the denizens of suburbia. It did briefly climb the horticultural social ladder during the nineteenth century, when it was accepted as a plant for the new fashion of summer bedding, but it never really established itself. When bedding began as a fashion for providing summer colour in a garden, the display might be changed two or three times during that season in large gardens. When the fashion settled down, May and June planting had to provide a display which would last until September – something which candytuft could not do. It is best suited to a brief, colourful display, and can be included in an annual border or as a filler for a herbaceous border or island bed; the rocket or hyacinth flowered types produce flowers on long stems which are useful for cutting. Candytuft is an easy plant for the novice to grow and it is one favoured by children – not the most patient of mortals. In their first gardens they want plants which grow quickly and are soon in flower; then, by the time they have tired of it, the candytuft is already over.

Candytuft is an annual and needs a place in full sun in a not too rich soil. Seed should be sown in parallel rows about 10in. (250mm) apart, with the resulting seedlings thinned to stand 6in. – 10in. (150–250mm) apart. Most seed catalogues offer a list of cvs that are white, purplish pink or red, and reach between 8in. (200mm) and 10in. (250mm) in height.

Castor Oil Plant

True events in life can on occasions be more extraordinary than fiction! A few years ago, *Ricinus communis* was in the news when a foreign diplomat was murdered in London by being stabbed in the leg by the ferule of an umbrella impregnated with a poison extracted from the castor oil plant. The public may well have been horrified by this story, but for children of earlier generations there was a different kind of horror associated with castor oil with which they were regularly dosed during the winter. Although best known as a medicine, castor oil has been used in the manufacture of soap and margarine, and as a lubricant, while Dioscorides advocated its use in lamps and for making candles; he also recommended it as a cure for sunburn. It was widely used by herbalists in sixteenth- and seventeenth-century England. At a time when plants cured by signature i.e. were believed to cure ailments of parts of the body suggested by the plants's shape, the shape of the leaves suggested that it would cure ailments of the hands: removing spots, bruises, burns and scars, and easing pains in the fingers caused by rheumatism. Other ailments against which it was claimed to be effective were dropsy, gout, and sciatica; oil poured into the ears was said to be a cure for earache and to improve the hearing; a lotion made from the leaves when applied to the eyes was thought to improve the sight of the elderly. As long as four hundred years ago the oil was used to dose children, but at this time it was used as a cure for worms.

In 1543 Leonart Fuchs, a German botanist, was saying in his herbal that, although a recent introduction, *Ricinus communis* was already common in gardens in his country, and five years later William Turner made a similar comment with respect to England although it was featured in Thomas Fromond's list of 1500. All the great gardeners of the seventeenth century were growing this plant, and although it was neglected in the following century it returned to favour in the nineteenth.

In the years after the Industrial Revolution in England manufacturers made fortunes in trade. These *nouveaux-riches* were keen to be accepted in the higher echelons of society, so they built large houses which were elaborately furnished and set in substantial gardens which had to be status symbols. At this time a glasshouse was considered to be *de rigeur*, and included amongst the tropical plants would be the handsome foliaged castor oil plant. The contents of these glasshouses would be ostentatiously planted outside in the garden during the summer months to be rehoused before the onset of cold weather in the autumn. This form of ostentation was to create a new garden fashion which came to be known as 'summer bedding'.

When the fashion started, beds laid out in a formal design would be filled with many different kinds of plants, but by the end of the century they had come to contain just a few varieties for mass display. Because edged ground cover tended to be rather flat, height was introduced by planting some tall dot-plants, and these might include caster oil plants. To provide novelty for the followers of this new fashion, seedsmen were offering many kinds of caster oil plants in their catalogues, ranging in height from 4ft to 10ft (1–3m) and with leaves of varying shades or red, bronze and green.

As *Ricinus communis* has been in cultivation for several hundred years; its country of origin is uncertain, for it is now widespread in most warm countries of the world, but North Africa seems the most likely. In warm countries it will grow into a tree of up to 40ft (10m) in height with a substantial trunk, but where winters are cold it can be treated as an annual. In one growing season, however, it can make considerable growth, and even in cold England 6ft (2m) is possible. Well spread alternate leaves on long stems are usually composed of seven lance-shaped leaflets with deeply serrated margins, each of which can exceed 10in. (250mm). Clusters of greenish flowers which are produced in late summer consist of yellowish males in the lower part and reddish females above. Following fertilisation, green fruits covered with soft green spines are produced, which when ripe split to eject three large shiny and attractively patterned seeds.

The specific epithet in *Ricinus communis* means common, whilst the generic name is the Latin word for a tick; perhaps there is a similarity of patterns on the seeds and parasites. Other names used in earlier centuries in England are derived from this parasite; in English 'tick-seed'; in Greek 'kroton'; and in Arabic, 'kiki'. The shape of the leaves produced the old botanical name of *Palma Christi* which became in English 'Christ's Palm' or 'hands of Christ'; 'castor oil plant', now the most common name was also the latest. According to Alphonse de Candolle, it came into use during the eighteenth century when large quantities of seed for oil were imported from Jamaica under the name of 'ango-casto', which became shortened and slightly altered to 'castor'. This seems to have been a Spanish or Portugese name intended for the chaste tree, *Vitex angus-castus*, so it would appear to have been a case of mis-identification.

As has been said, this plant is treated in English gardens as an annual. Although it can be sown directly into the garden, it takes so long to germinate that it is better started off under glass. If the glasshouse is provided with heat, seed can be sown in late winter or early spring; if it is unheated, wait until mid-spring when temperatures are rising. Seed is soaked in cold water for 24 hours before being pushed individually into a small pot of compost, soil or peat based. The length of time taken to germinate will depend on the temperature of the surroundings; the earliest sowings may need to be re-potted as the container fills with roots. Plant into a garden when the danger of frost has passed, amongst summer bedding for use as a filler in a herbaceous border, island bed or shrubbery, or in an annual border.

Catmint

The original plant to which this name applied was *Nepeta cataria*, a plant growing on chalk soil, common in Europe and extending into England. This vigorous and aromatic plant, which can reach 3ft (1m) in height, has opposite roundish, hairy, slightly grey-green leaves with a much-branched flower stem which produces large numbers of rather dingy white flowers, spotted with purple. Catmint, catnip, or just nep or nip, attracts cats from considerable distances to sniff, eat, rub against, roll on, jump in, or tear to pieces. In its presence cats seem to go berserk, in much the same way as some humans react to certain drugs; one rather prosaic explanation for this bizarre behaviour is that the oils contained in the plant have insecticidal properties. It was an early denizen of the English garden, taken there for its medicinal properties. Amongst the complaints that it was said to help were: colds in the head, catarrh, cramps, coughs and shortness of breath. One interesting virtue was that a meek person who chewed the root would become fierce and aggressive. Today the true catmint would be confined by an enthusiast to a herb garden, where it would be protected by a wire cage from the destruction inflicted upon it by cats.

Today catmint has come to be applied to another plant of the same genus and while it, too, is visited by cats, they do not wreak havoc to the same extent: this is *Nepeta X faasenii*. Count A. A. Mussin-Pushkin, who had been the Russian envoy in England and a friend of Sir Joseph Banks, sent natural history specimens back to his friend in England despite his own relative lack of interest in horticulture and botany. As a mineralogist, the count made expeditions to the Caucasus in his study of geology and sent seed and roots to Banks. Some of these proved to be hitherto undescribed plants; the best known of those which commemorate his name are: a pale blue spring-flowering bulb, *Pushkinia scilloides,* and *Nepeta mussinii.* It was this latter plant which was given the name 'catmint' when it came to be considered as an essential constituent of the new garden fashion of herbaceous borders introduced into English gardens by William Robinson during the last quarter of the nineteenth century. It was smaller than the original catmint but with showier spikes of lilac-coloured flowers produced in succession throughout the summer. It is, however, not the plant which we grow today as catmint.

N. X faassenii is a hybrid between *N. mussinii* and *N. nepetella,* originating in southern Europe. It almost certainly arose in a botanic garden as a chance seedling. In most botanic gardens, there are beds in which different genera and species of a plant family are grown together for student instruction. What seems to have happened is that these two species of *Nepeta* growing together in close proximity crossed with each other, and a resulting seedling survived. It is possible that this botanic garden was in Holland, and that the seedling was seen by the Dutch nurseryman J. H. Faassen during the last decade of the nineteenth century, who, recognising a good plant, propagated and distributed it. In any case, it soon came to replace *N. mussinii* in the garden, and it gained the affection of gardeners, which it still retains; it is to this plant that the name 'catmint' is applied today.

Nepeta X faassinii will tolerate most well drained soils and needs a position in full sun. Considered as an essential plant for the herbaceous border or island bed, it can be used to line a path or edge a bed and, as ground cover, is suitable for planting on steep banks, under hybrid tea and floribunda roses or amongst thinly planted shrubs. A plant produces a cluster of stems, square in cross-section with oval, toothed, slightly undulate margins on grey-felted leaves which are arranged in pairs, each pair at right angles to those above and below. In late spring these stems elongate to produce a much-branched flower stem of 18in. (450mm) with a large number of lilac-coloured flowers. There is a flowering season of about four weeks in early summer, and if the old stems are cut hard back as the display begins to fade, there will be a second flush of growth to provide autumn flowering. Propagation can be by division; plants are lifted in early spring before new growth has begun, pulled to pieces and each piece with roots is replanted; cuttings of non-flowering shoots taken in late summer are easy to root under some protection.

Celandine

This common name applies to two quite different plants; the lesser celandine is *Ranunculus ficaria* which belongs to the buttercup family, and the greater celandine, *Chelidonium majus,* to the poppy family. It is curious that *Ranunculus ficaria* has not been called buttercup or crowfoot as most species of *Ranunculus* are; could this be due to the differently shaped leaves, which are unlike most other species? Lesser celandine has a bunch of tubers, each about the size of a rice grain which are summer dormant and come into growth with the arrival of the autumn rains to produce a cluster of heart-shaped leaves of varying shades of green, sometimes bronze, which can be spotted. From amongst the leaves as winter comes to an end and spring begins, come buttercup-like flowers of many petals which are brownish below and bright yellow above; these close at night and in dull or wet weather. When it is cool, these flowers can last for several weeks; as the seeds begin to develop following fertilisation, the leaves turn yellow, and by the beginning of summer the aerial parts of the plant have died away. A plant that is common throughout Europe, comes into Britain, where it can be found in woodland, hedgerows, wet meadows and brightening up waste ground. It can grow as a weed in gardens and maybe troublesome if the soil is wet or of clay, because its tubers are so easily scattered during cultivation that no matter how carefully offending plants are dug out, some of the tiny tubers will be missed. Most plants which flower in the coldest season of the year are welcome, and as these plants have died down by the time summer arrives no one need worry about them except perhaps if they appear in the more formal areas of the garden.

In earlier centuries, plants were considered to 'cure by signature': a plant would effect a cure of any organ of the body it resembled. The tiny brown tubers resulted in the name of 'pilewort', by which it has long been known because it was said to cure this painful ailment. In some forms the leaves have prominent dots or marks, and a lotion made from them was used to remove spots or marks from the skin.

Four hundred years ago, when native plants were being introduced into the earliest English gardens, it was those forms which differed from the normal type that were grown; in the case of lesser celandines those with flowers that were paler or darker were in demand: cream or sulphur, and orange or bronze, as well as doubles of all these colours. These various forms, which are still with us, remained in cottage gardens until the nineteenth century, when they were given greater prominence by William Robinson, an indefatiguable writer, who recommended them for the herbaceous border, woodland and rock gardens. More recently, Reginald Farrer has included them in his *English Rock Garden* but with no great enthusiasm. Both Robinson and Farrer, as well as A. T. Johnson, mention a form with very large flowers for which they use the name – 'grandiflora': but does this still exist? The popularity of the celandine as a rock garden plant was not long-lived; possibly it was discarded to make room for an influx of more spectacular plants, but equally probably it was because it can become troublesome by spreading too freely. Even so, it provides a patch of brightness in late winter in a wild or woodland garden, in shade or where it is wet, and where it can be left to its own devices. The double flowered forms are better planted in isolation, for example amongst shrubs, but it is a good idea to mark their position so that their whereabouts are known when they are dormant, to prevent them from being disturbed by routine cultivation. Birds can be a problem in winter for they can destroy both leaves and flowers; protect the plants with wire-nettting or strands of black cotton stretched above the plants. The number of plants can be increased by dividing them as they pass out of flower.

The greater celandine is widespread throughout Europe, and although it does exist in England it is often found near habitation, suggesting that it has escaped from cultivation to naturalise in a few places. Its specific epithet is no doubt intended to separate it from the lesser celandine, whilst the generic name is derived from the Greek *chelodon* meaning 'a swallow', and it is the corruption of the Greek word which has produced 'celandine'. The Latin word for swallow is 'hirundaria', which has not only been an alternative common name, but was also used for a long time as a botanical name. Some 1500 years ago, Dioscorides called the plant *Chelidonia* because, he said, it came into growth with the arrival of the swallows; he added that when swallow fledgings were blind, the mother birds brought sprigs of the greater celandine to heal them.

A perennial plant which can reach 3ft (1m) in height, the greater celandine has alternate deeply lobed, hairy leaves which may be pale green, grey-green or blue-green; when stems or leaves are damaged they exude a sticky yellow sap. There is a branched flower stem with many small four-petalled yellow flowers followed by a quill-like seed pod. The plant was brought to this country by the Romans, and during the Dark Ages was cultivated in monastery gardens for use in medicine. With its yellow sap, the greater celandine was used to 'cure by signature' jaundice and other ailments of the liver, as Dioscorides had recorded. Even though its curing of blindness in swallows was a myth, it was nevertheless used for eye complaints in humans and was said to be effective in improving the vision of elderly people suffering from cataracts. It was used to relieve the discomfort caused by toothache, sunburn, itching and inflammation, and as a cure for other conditions of the skin: warts, running sores, ringworm and tetters (also known as tetterwort).

It may be a plant that an enthusiast would grow in a herb garden, but the celandine has little real beauty. Those forms whose leaves are bluish green have some attraction; there is also a variety known as *Laciniata* in which the leaves are finely cut, and another form has double flowers. The greater celandine is indifferent to soil as long as it is well drained and does not lie wet in winter; it grows on old walls and in the poorest of dry soils, where it remains smaller and tidier. In a normal garden soil it is a strong and untidy grower, with a tendency to swamp other more desirable plants. If it outgrows its allotted space it should be cut down to ground level, and it may then produce a second flush of growth. Self-sown seedlings usually appear on the singles and even occasionally from the double, whilst the laciniate forms come true from seed; if required, division can be practised in early spring before new growth begins.

— Chatham Island Forget~me~not —

In the nineteenth century, when forget-me-nots as we know them today became so common, they were left for the gardens of cottages, terraced houses or suburbia, for they were considered too mundane for the discriminating. This elite turned its attention to the newly arrived antipodean forget-me-nots which presented a challenge to grow and keep; instead of having blue flowers, they were mostly white, occasionally yellow, and even the colour of milk chocolate. On its arrival in England in 1849, the Chatham Island forget-me-not was welcomed, for here was a truly noble plant with flowers of the expected colour; even if these, like, all parts of the plant, were gigantic.

From a stout rootstock on long stems develop leaves resembling funnels, which may be round, oval, kidney or heart-shaped and in favourable conditions can reach or even exceed 12in. (300mm). Their upper surfaces are shiny, medium to dark shades of green and grooved, whilst the undersides are grey or silvery green with prominent ridged veins. In summer stout flower stems overtop the leaves with a flat or rounded head of many five-petalled flowers, paler on the outer edge but in a blue colour that intensifies as they age. Four winged nutlets follow the flowers, containing large, flat seeds ½ – ¾in. (12–18mm) in diameter.

On the Chatham Island this forget-me-not grows at the edge of the sea, in pockets of organic soil which results from decayed seaweed at the base of cliffs, or in sand along the high tide line, even being flooded at times by salt water. When it was discovered in 1840 by Dr Ernst Diffenbach, it was widespread and common, but now the grazing and trampling of animals have made it scarce, and it is on New Zealand's endangered plant list. Seed was brought back to the newly formed settlements on the two main New Zealand Islands, and to the growing towns in Australia, where it quickly became a popular garden plant. It was first described, in 1846, by J. D. Decaisne, director of Le Jardin des Plantes in Paris from a plant which had been grown in a garden, as *Myosotidium hortensia*. J. D. Hooker, who was to become director of Kew Gardens and who had collected specimens in the antipodes, used the name of *Cynoglossum nobile* when he described the plant for the *Gardeners' Chronicle* in 1858 but he must have changed his mind for in the following year in his description of the plant he gave it the botanical name *Myosotidium nobile*. *Myosotidium hortensia* remains the valid name, for this is the first that was published.

The English gentry seized upon this new and noble plant for their gardens, but they found it difficult to grow and it was not reliably hardy. It did, however, thrive in Devon and Cornwall, where the rainfall was higher, suiting the rhododendrons whose cultivation was developing into a new craze. These spectacular shrubs were attracting quite a following amongst the wealthy, who were sponsoring collectors to send back seed from the newly explored lands of the Far East. It was at this time that the Scottish lairds were planting woodland gardens on Scotland's western seaboard, where the annual rainfall could reach 100in. (2½m). To extend the late spring and early summer display provided by their rhododendrons, they were looking for other plants to grow with them which would also be attractive later in the deep shade produced by the often dense woodland canopy. They had found one group of suitable plants in the plantain lilies (now called *Hosta,* then known as *Funkia*) which were newly arrived from Japan. The plantain lilies, although producing attractive flowers, were being grown for their handsome leaves, and it was with these plants that the Chatham Island forget-me-not came to be grown primarily as a foliage plant. The owners of these Scottish estates would vie with each other to produce ever-larger leaves on their *Mysotidium hortensia* so that they could boast among themselves, even making wagers as to whose would be the largest.

In spite of what has been said, this plant is easier to grow than one might expect if a little effort is taken. It is not a plant for a cold garden, nor does it like summer drought either of soil or atmosphere. This is a plant for woodland in a lime-free soil which remains cool and moist during the summer and where if atmospheric humidity is low, it can be increased by irrigation (all conditions that one must consider when growing rhododendrons). Plants are occasionally offered for sale by specialist nurserymen, but seed is easier to find. The large seed is not long lived and should be sown as soon as it is obtained by inserting a single seed into a small container in a compost of equal parts of lime-free soil, sand and peat. Germination can be expected when in gentle heat after about four weeks, but there will always be a percentage of non-viable seed. Keep the seedlings growing in a shady position in a frost-free environment, re-potting before the plant becomes rootbound; plant out after the coldest part of the winter is over. Thoroughly prepare the gound by forking over and incorporating organic matter in the form of leafmould, well rotted compost or peat. Once it is planted an annual mulch is desirable in early spring, and because of the plant's maritime connections, seaweed is excellent material if available. The plants are especially prone to infestation by greenfly which can be seen most often on the underside of young leaves, but it is those which get down into the crown that cause the most severe damage: yellowing and distortion of newly emerged leaves which is not only unsightly but reduces the vigour of the plant and can even kill it.

When plants are raised from seed, the flower colours may vary amongst the many shades of blue, there can occasionally be an albino, and some flowers may be an unacceptable, even unpleasant, mauve in colour. Seed should never be collected from inferior forms, which, if the gardener is sufficiently strong willed, should be uprooted and consigned to the compost heap. Whenever seed is set on the best forms, some should be collected for immediate sowing. A succession of young plants should be aimed for, as the Chatham Island forget-me-not does not last long, especially when conditions are not ideal.

China Aster

This plant was called *Aster chinensis* by Linnaeus in *Species Plantarum*, but it was later reclassified as *Callistephus chinensis* by Ness von Essenbeck. To gardeners it will always be 'aster' without even its geographic adjective, whilst the true genus *Aster* will remain as 'Michaelmas daisy'. Father Pierre D'Incarville, a French missionary is credited with introducing this into Europe in 1728; however, he only joined the brotherhood of the Compagnie de Jesus in 1726, before undertaking prolonged training prior to going to Quebec where he stayed until 1735. If D'Incarville did introduce the plant it could not have been in 1728. It seems, though, that it was a French missionary who made the first introduction and sent seed to Antoine de Jussieu who was in charge of Le Jardin Botanique in Paris. Philip Miller, who was curator of the Chelsea Physic Garden, had had seed from Paris in 1731 from which he raised a red and a white flower, both singles, and from a second consignment of 1736 he raised a single blue flower. It was not until 1752 that he received seed from Dr Job Baster of Kirkzee in Holland which produced for him a red and a blue, both of which were double, and the following year another consignment of seed produced a double white. In 1771, the Reverend William Hanbury was growing red, white, blue and purple both as singles and doubles. Because the China aster flowered so late in British gardens, seed was infrequently set and so had to be imported from the warmer parts of France. James Justice in *The Scots Gardeners' Directory* of 1754 recommended sowing seed in the autumn and overwintering young plants under glass for planting out in spring, to produce an early summer flowering from which seed would be ripe by September.

The China aster was fashionable in France, where one of its names was 'Reine Marguerite', the 'queen of marguerites' or 'queen of daisies'. Horace Walpole records visiting one garden near Paris where he saw several thousand pots of China asters in flower. It must also have become popular in nineteenth-century Germany, where breeding was being carried out to produce an ever greater range of cultivars to sell in England, where the 'China aster' had become the 'German aster'. Towards the end of the nineteenth-century breeding seems to have crossed the Atlantic to the United States. By the first decade of the twentieth-century there were many groups of asters offered for sale by seedsmen under the following headings: Ray, Pompom or Liliput, Peony Flowered, Emperor, Victorian Jewel, Quilled, Giant Comet and Ostrich Plume; all reached 20–24ins. (500–600mm), but there was also a range of the same groups at half this height.

In 1824, Henry Phillips in *Flora Historica* was advocating following spring flowering bulbs with China asters raised on hot beds from which they were transferred to the flower garden by means of a transplanter. This is an early mention of the new fashion of summer bedding which was beginning to attract a following. China asters were to remain firm favourites as summer bedding subjects, and as they did not flower until late summer or autumn they were suitable plants to follow late flowering spring bedding, such as Dutch iris, Sweet William and Canterbury bells. In the garden they had a place in an annual border, or they could be used as fillers in the herbaceous border, island beds or amongst shrubs. They have long been in demand as cut flowers either bought from the florists or taken from the garden.

In the years which followed the Second World War fungus diseases began to attack China asters with increasing severity so that fewer and fewer seedlings survived to flower, and it seemed as though they were doomed. Plant breeding saved the day; after some 30 years resistant strains have been bred and now, in the 1980s, China aster can once again be grown, although in fewer varieties than were available 50 years ago.

Seed should be sown under the protection of a frost-free house in mid spring and seedlings pricked out as soon as they are big enough to handle into boxes of soil or peat based compost, 2in. (50mm) apart. Plant them out where they are to flower as soon as the leaves are touching in the box. In areas where summers are warm, direct sowings can be made, although from these later flowering should be expected.

—— Christmas Rose ——

Helleborus niger is to be found in deciduous woodland on a chalk soil on the lower mountain slopes of several countries of southern and central Europe, including Germany, Switzerland, Italy and Yugoslavia. This evergreen perennial has dark green leaves composed of several leaflets, wedge-shaped at the base, more or less oblong in outline and with few serrations; the basal pair of leaflets may be deeply lobed. Flowering can take place at any time from mid autumn until late spring, although midwinter flowering is considered most desirable; flowers are followed by a group of seven seed capsules. *H. niger* ssp *macranthus*, which occurs in northern Yugoslavia and Italy, has broader leaflets, lance-shaped in outline and more bluish grey in colour, with a greater number of serrations and stiffer in texture; flowers are much larger but on shorter stems and tend to appear in late winter or early spring.

The generic name, the same as that used by the ancients, is derived from a Greek word meaning 'poisonous' or 'deadly', whilst the specific epithet meaning 'black' refers to the colour of the roots. 'black hellebore', the earliest English name, was a general name, and whilst it included *H. niger* it referred also to a number of other species; to differentiate it from the others it came to be called 'true black hellebore'. It has a long history of cultivation in Europe and appeared in the *Materia Medica* of Dioscorides, written about 500 AD. Already, 1500 years ago, this plant had long been in cultivation, for one can read: 'it is called *Melampodium* since it is thought that one Melampus, a goatherd did thereby first purge ye daughters of

Proteus being mad; when they dig it they stand praying to Apollo and Aesculapeus observing ye eagles flight for ye bird causeth death if so he see ye digging of ye hellebore; but one must dig with all celerity because there is a headache caused by the exhalation; hence for prevention, they which dig it, eat garlick and drink wine'. For many centuries it was planted near a house to provide protection against thunderbolts and demons. Bunches of flowers and/or leaves were hung around the necks of cattle to protect against the evil eye. While Dioscorides had used black hellebore to cure epilepsy, melancholy, arthritis, paralysis, leprosy and toothache, Gerard was saying, 'a purgation of Hellebore is good for mad and furious men' and William Cole used it against dropsy, scabs, leprosy, cancer, scald-head or scurf, eliphancy and such foul diseases of the skin.

The black hellebore was brought to England by the Romans and it survived their departure in monastery gardens. It was known to William Turner in 1538, who called it 'bearfoot'. Just as 'black hellebore' had referred to more than one plant, so too did 'bearfoot', and today we retain this name for *H. foetidus*. Most common names have been associated with the time of flowering: winter rose, Christmaswort, Christmas flower and Christmas herb; it has also been called Christ's flower and Saint Agnes flower, after the saint to whom it is dedicated. The first mention of Christmas rose seems to be in *Flora, Ceres and Pomona* by John Rea, in 1665.

This is one of a few garden plants which has remained in favour with gardeners throughout the centuries, even if it has been more prized in cottage gardens than in those of the wealthy. Any plant which is in flower in northern European gardens in midwinter must be regarded with special favour. For a plant that has been in cultivation throughout the countries of Europe for some 3000 years there has been remarkably little variation. The earliest variant is one mentioned by John Tradescant the younger in his list of the plants in his garden at Lambeth in 1658; he described it as an early flowering Christmas rose, a form which still exists today. A number of forms have been offered for sale by nurserymen in the twentieth century, the varieties based mainly on flower size, while some seem to be pink-tinged, especially on the outside of the petals. With growers selecting varieties for flower size and perhaps stem length, less attention has been paid to the time of flowering, and fewer and fewer cvs or selections now seem to flower at Christmas. Possibly the best of recent introduction is 'Potters Wheel', probably bred from *H. niger* ssp *macranthus,* which has flowers 4in. (100mm) in diameter but is of rather weak constitution, and Lewis Cobbet, which has rose-pink shading on the outside of the petals. *H. niger* has been crossed with *H. lividus corsicus* to produce *H. Xnigricors.* This hybrid, which is a cross between a caulescent and an acaulescent species, produces its greenish cream flowers first from the aerial stem, followed by flowers of the same colour direct from the rootstock; flowering takes place during midwinter.

Although the Christmas rose prefers the light shade of trees or shrubs, it seems well suited to growing in full exposure. A heavier soil containing lime suits it better than a light soil, but in any kind of soil organic matter should be incorporated and applied as an annual mulch. For introducing the plant into a garden, those which have been container grown are better than bare-rooted; plant in early spring before new growth commences. Do be patient, for it can take a year or two for new plants to settle down and begin to grow and flower regularly. A sheet of glass fixed above the clump when flower buds are first seen will ensure that the opening blooms remain unmarked by mud splashes. The newly emerging flower buds are prone to attack by slugs and snails; their ravages can be guarded against by scattering slug pellets around.

Because of the time of flowering, when weather conditions are bad and pollinating insects are few, seed is set only infrequently. If there is seed available, this should be gathered as the capsules are splitting and the seed sown immediately, whilst seed which falls to the ground will germinate freely almost a year hence. Seed which is collected and allowed to dry rarely or only poorly germinates. When immediate sowing is not possible, store the seed in moist peat, sand or sphagnum moss. Well established clumps can be increased by division, immediately after flowering. Carefully lift the clump and cut it into two or four pieces, ensuring that there are plenty of roots on each, and replant into well-prepared ground.

When *H. niger* in the northern hemisphere flowers at the festive season, gardens are virtually bare of flowers, so its blooms are much in demand for decorating the house. Flowers of the Christmas rose must be put into water immediately they are picked, when they will last for two or three weeks in a cool room; if there is any delay the flowers wilt and will not recover.

Common Jasmine

The common jasmine is so called not because it is the most frequently grown species in gardens today, but because it has been longest in cultivation. There are but a few names for this plant, in addition to 'white jasmine'; the others are corruptions of it, or alternative spellings: jessamine, gessamine, gethsamine, gelsemine and gesse or jesse. In *Beals Trees and Shrubs Hardy in the British Isles,* distribution of *Jasminum officinale* is given as: the Caucasus, northern Persia, Afghanistan, the Himalaya and China. As the plant was known to all the ancient civilisations, it may be that its wide distribution results from escapes from cultivation, so that one can only speculate on its true country of origin.

According to William Turner it was well established in gardens in England by the mid-sixteenth century, and was known and written about by all the famous gardeners of the seventeenth. It remained fashionable in the eighteenth century, despite being banished to the kitchen garden, and its fragrant flowers have ensured its survival to the present day, athough it has long languished in the obscurity of cottage gardens. Of all the senses, that of smell is most closely associated with nostalgia; it conjures up memories of country gardens of yesteryear on warm sunny, summer days when as a child one visited elderly relatives. Four hundred years ago Gerard was recommending the planting of this jasmine against arbours and banqueting houses, while in 1659, Sir Thomas Hanmer was using it as an understock on which to graft new and tender species, and in 1728 Batty Langley was expressing abhorrence of jasmines trained as weeping standards.

Oil of jasmine has long been considered a perfume while jasmine butter, which was made by mixing flowers with butter or lard, was used by ladies for rubbing on leather gloves to soften and perfume them; an infusion of the flowers was used in bathing and for removing body odours. Gerard recommended boiling jasmine leaves in wine to make a poultice to reduce swellings, while John Peachey says, 'the oyl of it heals, mollifies and opens; and is used in contractions of limbs and like'. The fragrance of jasmine flowers in a closed room can be overpowering, according to Gilbert White writing in his journal, and at the end of the sixteenth century, John Gerard was saying, 'in those of a hot constitution it causeth headache and the overmuch smell therof maketh the nose to bleed'. Jasmine has long been used for adornment by ladies in garlands, posies and nosegays. It has been featured in wedding ceremonies and in some countries the inclusion of jasmine flowers in a wedding bouquet was an indication of the wealth and status of the bride's family.

This jasmine is not a plant for a cold garden, for although it is surprisingly hardy, there is always freer and more copious flowering in gardens in areas where summers are warm and sunny. As long ago as 1659, Sir Thomas Hanmer was recommending that it be planted against a south or west wall, because in such a position the additional warmth encouraged better flowering. It is largely indifferent to soil, but avoid one that is too rich, otherwise it will make excessive growth at the expense of flowering. When choosing a position in which to plant jasmine, make sure that the wall is high enough and that it has enough lateral space to spread, for it is a vigorous grower. Some support is necessary in the form of parallel wires or a wooden trellis, which should be strong enough to support hefty stems which become both thick and heavy with age. Plant from a container when the danger of frost is over, and train in the stems in the early years, ensuring that the lower part of the wall is well clothed and remains so. Some pruning is desirable in spring once the risk of frost has passed; reduce excessive growth, shorten back shoots coming away from the wall, thin crowded stems and remove weak growth. Old gardening books recommend layering as a means of propagation; this consists of pegging down low-growing stems of previous seasons' growth in early spring before new growth begins. Cuttings taken of shoots which have completed their growth in mid-summer are not difficult to root under some protection.

The ordinary species, only occasionally offered for sale by nurseries, can be shy flowering with blooms which are pure white. *Jasminum officinale affine,* the form most commonly offered for sale, is pink in the bud but pure white when the flowers are open and is said to be more free flowering than the straight species. This form was introduced into England by Dr John F. Royle in about 1840, who had been a medical superintendent to the East India Company, and the director of its botanic garden. *J. officinale 'Aurea'* has leaves which are blotched with yellow, providing additional summer interest. It is just as vigorous as the straight species, and whilst not everyone cares for variegated plants (in this instance the variegation is virus induced), it flowers much more freely than any of the other forms grown in English gardens. Together with another variety having silver variegation, *J. officinale 'Aurea'* was grown by Philip Miller in the Chelsea Physic Gardens in 1738. He describes both these forms as being tender, and although that may explain why a silver variegated jasmine is no longer with us, his assessment for the golden one was incorrect, for it is quite hardy in the south of England.

Convolvulus Tricolor

Convolvulus is a name which strikes terror into the hearts of most gardeners, for it is associated with noxious weeds which, once established in a garden, are almost impossible to eradicate. Originally 'convolvulus' as a common name was an alternative name for two plants, the lesser bindweed, *Convolvulus arvensis,* and the great bindweed, *C. sepium,* although the latter has been transferred to the genus *Calystegia.* Both these plants can be admired in hedgerows, on the fringes of woodland and on fences around waste ground, for they have large showy, white, occasionally pink trumpet-shaped flowers. Unfortunately, however, both plants have long creeping underground stems which invade our gardens sending up shoots to strangle the plants we are trying to grow. It is not enough just to pull them up, for what remains in the ground just grows away again: care must be exercised when digging up these underground stems, for every remaining stem will grow into another plant. It is unfortunate that the antics of these two species have blackened the name of convolvulus for gardeners, for it is a genus with many attractive flowering species.

It is odd that the English, who have an aversion to foreign words have retained the botanical name for this plant, rather than coming up with some English name. When it first came into England it was variously known as 'lesser blue bindweed', 'lesser Spanish bindweed' or 'small blue convolvulus'. It was discovered by Gulliame Boel growing in Spain and Portugal in 1608, he sent seed to both William Coys and John Parkinson. While it was unknown to Gerard, Thomas Johnson included it in his revision of the *Herbal* of 1633; it is in the 1658 list of plants growing in John Tradescant's garden at Lambeth, and it was offered for sale in William Lucas's catalogue of 1677. It was much grown in English gardens, but it may well have been even more popular in Holland for it became a plant that was often featured in the flower paintings of the seventeenth and eighteenth centuries; the English artist James Furber and the Dutch artist Jacob van Huysum both included it in their works.

Convolvulus tricolor is a low growing, rather sprawling annual which, like most species of convolvulus, closes its flowers at night or in dull or wet weather. The flowers, except when it is dull, last only for a day and in very hot weather they may already have shrivelled or closed by early afternoon. In 1771, the Reverend William Hanbury wrote 'This species goes by the name of The Life of Man; it having flower buds in the morning, which will be in full bloom by noon and withered before night'.

Although the flowers are short lived, they are produced in succession throughout the summer. This plant, while not amongst the most fashionable, has always kept its place in the garden because it provides flowers that are predominantly a good rich blue, the rarest of summer flower colours. In the twentieth century, it has been used in bedding in an annual border, and as a filler in an island bed, herbaceous border or shrubbery.

Choose a position in a not over-rich soil in full sunlight sow the seed in parallel rows about 12in. (300mm) apart during early spring, and just cover, later thinning the resulting seedlings to the same distance apart. Seedlings raised under glass can after being pricked out, be planted into permanent positions as soon as they are big enough. Earlier flowering can be obtained by sowing seeds in the previous autumn and allowing the young plants to overwinter.

While the flower colour of the species which was first introduced is marine blue with a white throat and yellow base or eye (the three colours of the specific epithet), gardeners are always looking for novelty, and seed catalogues offer pink, red, violet and pure white varieties as well as white with stripes, either with entire edges or fringed, in addition there are forms which are dwarfer or more compact.

———— Cotton Thistle ————

This biennial, which extends throughout Europe is found in scattered localities throughout Britain; it may be a native plant, although it has been suggested that it has become naturalised following its introduction as impurities amongst grain and other farm seeds imported from the continent. In its first year it forms a large but loose rosette of oblong or lance-shaped leaves with large teeth which taper to a sharp point. The leaves and the entire plant are covered with a cottony wool. In the second year a stout stem arises from the centre of the rosette, sometimes exceeding 6ft (2m). This angled stem, which has lines of prominent spines along its edges, branches out in its upper part with each branch terminating in a large, spiny thistle-like head from which emerge reddish purple flowers. This is an impressive plant and is well worth a place in a garden when space is available: at the back of a herbaceous border, in the centre of an island bed or grouped amongst shrubs. The large seed can be space sown where the plants are to flower; thereafter the plants can be left to their own devices, for they will self-sow. All that is necessary is to ensure that only a few seedlings are allowed to remain.

Over the years the cotton thistle has had two other generic names: *Acanthium* and *Cirsium*; its valid name, however, is *Onopordon acanthium*. In English there are or have been, many common names, some of which are: 'white cotton thistle', 'white woolly thistle', 'woolly thistle', wild white thistle', 'ote thistle', 'argentine thistle' and 'silver thistle'. William Turner knew this plant in 1548, but only from gardens, whereas John

Gerard describes it as growing by the wayside. Thomas Johnson, who was responsible for the 1633 revision of Gerard's *Herbal,* had been with a party from the Society of Apothecaries on a botanical trip in 1632, and he records that they found it on the Isle of Thanet. There are few records of its deliberate cultivation during the seventeenth century, and Philip Miller, writing in *The Gardener's Dictionary* of 1768 was not attracted to it and warned that it often became a troublesome weed. The Reverend William Hanbury writing three years later in *Complete Body of Gardening and Planting,* held it in greater esteem as a garden plant, and mentions that he had a form which had white flower. Today it is one of the many plants that have been claimed as the true Scots thistle, a myth fostered by the corporation of Edinburgh who have made extensive plantings in Princes Street gardens which are in flower at Festival Time. Amongst the plants which have been considered to be the Scots thistle are: cardoon (*Cynara cardunculus*), globe thistle (*Echinops ritro*) and various species of *Cirsium* and *Carduus.* The reason given for the Scots choosing a thistle for their emblem is based on a story of the time of Malcolm I. Norsemen invading Scotland, besieging Staines Castle, decided one night to make a surprise attack across the almost dry moat. In the middle of the night they removed their footwear so that they could advance silently, but, unknown to them, the moat was filled with thistles and when the invaders trod on these, their yells and curses alerted the defenders and the enemy was routed. Like so many myths there can be little truth in this one. The cotton thistle, which is in fact rare in Scotland, occurs as an occasional plant and never in quantity; however dark the night, no one could have accidentally trodden on a plant which at flowering can be 6ft (2m) high. This story may well be apocryphal, but if there is a vestige of truth in it then what plant was the thistle? There is no doubt that the flower depicted in heraldic devices is a thistle, and there is some resemblance to the head of the cotton thistle, but even so it could be any one of a number of others and may be just an artistic impression. *Cirsium vulgare,* the spear thistle, seems to have the best claim, although a Dr Johnson said that *Carduus nutans,* the musk thistle was a strong contender while he personally favoured *Carduus marianus,* the blessed thistle.

Creeping Jenny

In the botanical name for this plant, *Lysimachia nummularia,* the genus may commemorate King Lysimachos, a ruler of ancient Thrace, although there is also a Greek word *lysimachos* which refers to terminating a war or ending strife, which seems the more likely when loose strife is a general name for plants of this genus. The specific epithet is derived from a Latin word which means 'resembling a coin', which is indicated also by some of its common names: 'moneywort', 'twopennywort', 'herb-two-pence', 'herb tuppence', 'twopenny grass'. Its habit of growth has provided: 'running Jenny', 'creeping Joan', 'creeping Charlie' or 'creeping (yellow) loosestrife'.

Creeping Jenny is widespread throughout southern Europe and occurs in England and Wales, but not in Scotland. It frequents damp soil under deciduous woodland, in water meadows or along the banks of streams and rivers. It has thin, soft stems which can grow up to 3ft (1m) in length in one season, having opposite, almost round leaves from whose axils arise small cup-shaped yellow flowers.

For centuries it has been a favourite plant of country folk and was taken into gardens several hundred years ago largely for its curative properties, at a time when garden plants had to be useful rather than decorative. Some of its uses were: to staunch bleeding (both externally and internally), clear up ulcers, provide a cough cure for children, strengthen the stomach, cure dropsy, prevent or stop vomiting, and as a herb tea it was given to ladies who tended to swoon.

During the eighteenth and early nineteenth centuries it seems to have gone out of favour and was little grown in gardens, but when it did return to favour in the middle of the nineteenth century, it was as a flowering plant instead of a medicinal herb. In London, it came to be grown in window boxes, where it was allowed to droop over the edges, and it became a popular plant for hanging baskets in unheated conservatories where its long, thin stems could cascade towards the ground. William Sutherland in his *Hardy Herbaceous and Alpine Plants* of 1871 says, 'It is useful for a variety of purposes – for clothing rockwork, moist banks, front lines in mixed beds and borders, and for festooning the margins of rustic vases where such ornaments may with propriety of taste be introduced into flower gardens'.

Both Sutherland and William Robinson mention a creeping Jenny with variegated leaves, and it was during the 1870s, that the golden leaf form was introduced. In the present day any of the forms make an effective ground cover under rhododendrons, for they revel in the cool conditions and moist soil, flowering very freely in the shade. The shallow rooting of creeping Jenny ensures that the plant does not compete for water, nor does it hinder the penetration of rain. The golden leaf form can be used in bedding, and is especially useful in shade; it is effective as an edging or ground cover through which another plant can grow such as a dwarf form of heliotrope or a blue lobelia or ageratum. As the plant roots as it grows, it is easily increased by lifting a clump at almost any time, (although early spring is best), pulling apart and replanting rooted pieces.

Crown Imperial

The crown imperial has a large naked bulb from which emerges a stout stem, rising on occasions to 3ft (1m), with tiered whorls of lance-shaped leaves which, when bruised, emit an unpleasant fox-like smell. At the top of the stem a number of pendulous cup-shaped flowers will develop through which will poke a tuft of upright green leaves. The earliest kinds grown in European gardens were orange, resembling medieval gold crowns, which resulted in the botanical name of *Corona imperialis* which was anglicised to 'crown imperial'. An alternative botanical name was *Lilium byzantinum* because it was considered to be a lily. In *Species Plantarum*, (1753) Linnaeus classified it as *Fritillaria imperialis*. The generic name is derived from the Latin word *fritillus,* which was the word for a dice box used by Roman soldiers when gambling. Two alternative reasons are given for this derivation: the seed pod resembles the dice box in shape; as do the flowers of some species especially those of the snake's head lily, *F. meleagris.*

Fritillaria imperialis grows wild in a number of countries at the western end of the Himalayas; namely, India, Russia, Afghanistan and Persia, from where it was introduced into Turkey. It was seen in the sixteenth century growing in the gardens of Suleiman the Magnificent at Constantinople by Ogier Ghislain de Busbeq who was an ambassador to the Byzantine court. He included it with tulips, hyacinths and Asian ranunculus in the diplomatic bag which he sent back to his master Ferdinand I in about 1550. A single orange form was common in Gerard's garden at Holborn in 1596, and he also grew what he called a rare double. Parkinson was so impressed with this plant that he used it to introduce readers to his book *Paradisus in Sole,* which was published in 1629; 'The Crowne Imperiall for his stately beautifulness deserveth the first place in this our garden of Delight'. Sir Thomas Hanmer, 30 years later, did not have the same enthusiasm for it; 'The sorts of them are only three, which are: The Ordinary Single Orange, of an ill dead colour, The Double Orange, yet rare, The Single Yellow, more rare'. In 1706 in an English translation of the *Compleat Florist* one reads of a deep red, the colour of a boiled lobster and a single with a faint red flower, half of which is a reddish yellow 'not to be despised'. It must have been the eighteenth century when the crown imperial became a fashionable garden plant. Philip Miller in the 1768 edition of his *Gardener's Dictionary* listed 12 kinds, which included striped flowers, doubles, others with multiple tiers and two with variegated foliage. Three years later in *The Universal Botanist and Nurseryman,* Richard Weston adds one with a branched flower stem, another that was fasciated and one described as scentless. Could this refer to the fox-like smell of the bruised leaves? A geographical form, *F. imperialis inodora* was collected by Albert Regel about 1884 in south east Turkestan, and sent to the gardens of St Petrograd. It is described as being without the usual foxy smell of the species, and herbarium specimens seem identical with *F. eduardii*.

Although cultivation of crown imperial declined towards the end of the eighteenth century there was a resurgence during the second half of the nineteenth. Bulbs of all kinds became immensely fashionable and to supply an ever-increasing demand, nurserymen were looking for novelties and new plants by sponsoring plant collectors to search all over Europe and Asia Minor. In catalogues published up to the Second World War there were large numbers of crown imperials offered, although the difference between them seems to have been slight. Today the interest in bulbs continues, but more among the small growing kinds that are suited to rock garden or alpine house cultivation. Although since the Second World War many species of *Fritillaria* new to cultivation have arrived in this country, most have proved less than easy to grow and, while the *cognoscenti* use their skills to attempt their cultivation the old crown imperial has gone out of favour.

Crown imperial is the tallest species, has the largest flowers and while it is the most impressive, it is also the easiest to grow. Once established in a garden it is best left alone and only lifted and replanted when it becomes overcrowded or begins to decline. Bulbs should be lifted whilst the stems are visible but when the leaves have turned yellow. Lift carefully with a fork, taking care not to skewer the bulbs, pull apart and replant immediately. If there has to be a delay, store the bulbs in moist sand or peat.

Bulbs will be on sale in the autumn for those who want to introduce them to their garden, but the customer should inspect them before buying to ensure that the scales are not dry or extensively bruised and that there are plenty of living roots attached to the base; bulbs without roots are difficult and very slow to establish. Select a piece of ground that is well drained, and incorporate plenty of well rotted compost, leaf mould or peat, plant on a firm base with the tips of the bulbs 4in. (100mm) below ground level. An annual mulch of the same kinds of organic matter is beneficial when applied in spring, after the frost has left the ground but before the shoots emerge.

Late spring frosts may damage shoots which appear through the ground early; these damaged shoots are prone to infection by the grey-mould fungus (*Botrytis cinerea*) which if not controlled can spread down the stem, infect the bulb and cause its death. Immediately this disease is seen, spray with a fungicide containing copper. Slugs and snails are the most serious pests, for these chew at the emerging shoots or tunnel into more developed stems. These tend to be more of a problem when there is a

47

lot of weed growth, so make sure that the ground remains clean and scatter slug pellets over the ground as the shoots emerge.

Bulbs can be increased by lifting clumps as the stems begin to yellow, and pulling apart. Keep the largest bulbs to replant for immediate flowering, while the smaller ones should be lined out in a nursery bed and grown on until they reach flowering size. As seed is set in most years, this is another method of increase but it will take more than three years from sowing to flowering. As the seed capsule splits, take it off the plant with a portion of stem and cover with a paper bag; hang it upside-down in a warm place until the seed has fallen out of the capsules. Sow directly in a cold frame, just covering the seeds, and leave without protection over the winter; germination will take place as the temperature rises in the spring. Seed sown in boxes can be stood in a glasshouse for two or three weeks until the radicle emerges; then the box is taken outside and left exposed to the winter's cold and germination will occur in the following spring. Space out seedlings the following year in a nursery bed as the tiny bulbils begin to grow, in a nursery bed.

Daisy

Many weeds can be unpleasant, invasive and difficult to control and every effort is made to eliminate them; others, in small numbers or of improved selections, can be pleasing and are retained in a garden. The common daisy can fit into either category, depending on taste! When they are present in a lawn in quantity, the orderly gardener sets about their destruction, although the non-purist may consider daisy-sprinkled grass a pleasing sight. Even if the daisy is considered a weed, it does have common appeal and was long ago taken into gardens, keeping its popularity more in a cottage than in a grand garden.

Candytuft, Iberis umbellata

Castor Oil Plant, Ricinus communis

Modern cultivars of Convolvulus tricolor

Monstrosum form of Common Daisy used in bedding

There seem to be three possible sources of derivation for the generic name in *Bellis perennis; bellus* – beautiful; *bellum* – war (the leaves of the daisy were used to staunch bleeding); Belides – a Greek dryad who was transformed into a flower to protect her from the lecherous advances of the god Vertumnus. The daisy has a golden eye surrounded by a ring of petals, white above and entirely, or tipped with, pink or red beneath. At night these petals close, reopening during the day to expose their centre or eye, hence 'days-eyes' which became 'daisies'.

The daisy has long been a symbol of purity, and in Celtic mythology, it was the flower of the new born and became the emblem of fidelity and innocence; it has also been associated with children, who pick the flowers to make posies or daisy chains. While it has mostly been associated with the common folk, it was looked upon with favour by three royal ladies, all called Margaret: Margaret of Anjou, wife of Henry VI of England; the sister of the French king, Francis I; the wife of Prince Humbert, the first king of a united Italy. Marguerite, the French word for Margaret, has become a general name in both France and England for may kinds of daisies.

Over the centuries, poets have waxed lyrical about the common daisy.

By dimpled brook and fountain brim
The wood-nymphs, deck'd with Daisies trim
Their merry wakes and pastimes keep.

The medieval poet Geoffrey Chancer wrote: while three centuries later, John Milton was writing:

Of all the floures in the mede,
Than love I most these floures white and rede
Such that men callen daisies in our town
To them I have so great affectioun.

Shakespeare, of course, has references to the daisy:

Without the bed her other fair hand was
On the green coverlet, whose perfect white
Sowed like an April daisy on the grass

as does the Romantic poet William Wordsworth:

Most pleased when most uneasy;
But now my own delights I make
My thirst at every rill can slake
And gladly nature's love partake
Of thee, sweet daisy

It became a garden plant more than 400 years ago when plants grown in a garden had to be useful. Fresh daisy flowers were added to salads for decoration, although they were also eaten. A poultice of leaves was used to alleviate the pain, and to remove the discolouration of bumps and bruises. Pounded leaves made into an ointment by mixing them in unsalted butter was used on parts of the body afflicted with gout. Gerard, in his *Herbal* wrote: 'The juyce of the leaves snift up into the nostril purgeth the head mightily of foule and filthy slimie humours and helpeth the megrim (migraine) . . . The same given to little dogs with milke, keepeth them from growing big'.

Gardening books throughout the seventeenth century mention many kinds of daisy; single and double varieties which were white, pink, red, speckled, striped and with petals having each side of a different colour; one with a green flower was described as 'rare'. A novelty, known as the 'childing' or 'hen-and-chickens' daisy had a normal double flower from which developed a ring of tinier flowers, also double. Except for the green form, many, if not most, of these can be found today. In these earlier books are illustrations that closely resemble the monstrosum and pomponette groups offered in present-day seed catalogues. In England, after the Second World War, two miniature forms were offered for sale by nurserymen as rock garden plants: the pink 'Dresden China' and the red 'Rob Roy', which are similar to some of the old woodcuts. Neither of them was long lived, and nor was their appeal – one has to really search to find them today.

Any of the smaller flowered, named cvs can be used in the rock garden, with the larger and stronger forms along the edge of paths or beds; these need to be lifted every second or third year after the spring flowering and divided. The monstrosum and pomponette, which are raised from seed sown in late summer, will provide plants of autumn planting for spring bedding. All the pomponettes look well with any species of *Muscari*, but especially *M. armeniacum* 'Blue Spike' and the monstrosum types go best with a dwarf tulip such as *Tulipa fosteriana* 'Princeps'.

Dog Tooth~violet

Erythronium dens-canis occurs wild in woodlands on lower mountain slopes throughout Europe and Asia and extends into Japan, although some of the geographic forms have been given specific rank by botanists. Belonging to the lily family, dog tooth-violet has a white bulb which is summer dormant, coming into growth in late autumn or winter to produce a single lance-shaped leaf when immature, but when it is about to flower there are a pair of leaves which are heavily spotted or blotched with purple. In early spring the stems measuring up to 8in (200mm), end in flowers with swept-back petals of a purplish pink colour. By the time the seed capsule has ripened and scattered its seed the leaves have turned yellow and died away.

The generic name is derived from two Greek words: *erythros* – red, and *ion* – violet. In English, 'red violet' may seem a strange name for a plant when the majority of species, concentrated along the Pacific seaboard of North America, are yellow and pink; but red was the colour of the flowers of the first known species. In earlier centuries violet was a more general name than it is today for it included such plants as snowdrops, wallflower, honesty and lupin. The specific epithet, once the botanical name (sometimes *dens caninus*) which in English became 'dogtooth', refers to the shape of the bulb. Although 400 years ago the present-day common name was used, it was more usually referred to simply as 'dog's tooth'.

The flower is recorded as a recent introduction to John Gerard's garden at Holborn in 1597, and it is said to have been brought into England by his rival Mathias L'Obel for his master Lord Edward Zouche, who had a garden at Hackney. At that time Gerard was growing two kinds: purple or flesh-coloured, and white. Thirty-two years later John Parkinson had one other colour in his garden at Long Acre, as did John Rea in 1665 who also had one with a yellow flower at Kinlet in Shropshire: this was *E. americanum* which was being grown by John Tradescant at Lambeth in 1633; No gardener of the seventeenth century mentions a red variety, nor did Philip Miller as late as 1768; perhaps most felt that this so-called form differed too little from the usual purplish pink to warrant distinguishing it. The Reverend William Hanbury in 1771 and Mawe and Abercrombie in 1797 had no hesitation in differentiating four shades of red with narrow, and four with broad leaves; together with two white forms they grew ten different kinds. In the following two hundred years there seem to have been only purplish pink and white grown. It is interesting to note in the 1837 catalogue of Flannagan and Nutting, who had a nursery in London by the Mansion House, that the purple, now the most common form, was selling for 10/- (50p) a dozen while the now rarer white could be bought for 4/- (20p) a dozen. The dogtooth-violet began to fall from favour during the nineteenth century, an unexpected development considering that the new fashion of rock gardening was beginning to gather strength. In 1870 William Robinson wrote that it was 'one of the loveliest of all our old garden flowers, now seldom seen though it should be in every place where spring flowers are welcome'. Readers of books written by Reginald Farrer were accustomed to his barbed comments about plants which were not amongst those he prized most highly; in *The English Rock Garden* he wrote: 'The Dog's-Tooth Violets are amongst the most precious and exquisite things for spring flowering – not by any means duly realised in gardens where *E. dens-canis,* very pretty, but the least striking, perhaps of all, is often only to be seen and that only because it survives from the enthusiasm of Parkinson's day'.

Sir Thomas Hanmer said in *The Garden Book*, 'They love a rich earth and a warm place, and endure not to bee long out of the ground'; in *Flora, Ceres and Pomona* by John Rea is the comment, 'many of them are brought over out of France and Flanders by such as make a trade of selling flowers, whereof there are many now about London, but commonly they are over so late, that not one ten of them will grow'. These two observations made more than 300 years ago are interesting, even though Rea is not correct in his reasoning. Bulbs of dogtooth-violet, once out of the ground, need to be stored in moist peat or sand to keep scales plump and roots from shrivelling. When bulbs have been allowed to dry out so that the roots are dead, if they do survive replanting, they take a long time to establish themselves and grow away. Bulbs bought for planting should be in the pots in which they were raised, and even these may abort their flowers in the year following planting. Once planted, clumps of bulbs should be left undisturbed until they become overcrowded or flowering begins to decline. Lift the dormant bulbs carefully, for they can be very deep in the soil, separate them, remove off-sets and replant as soon as possible. The soil into which dogtooth-violets are to be planted should have large quantities of organic matter incorporated. Unlike the North American species which demands an acid soil, *E. dens-canis* grows equally well on one containing lime.

Although dogtooth-violets will grow well in a not too dry soil in full sun, they are better in light shade, such as a shrub border, or naturalised in a woodland garden; make sure that the soil is bare, for they do not seem able to compete with other vegetation. Bulbs can be containerised for flowering in an alpine house using a soil based compost. Reduce watering after the flowers are over but do not allow the soil to become dust dry; in late summer remove the soil down to the level of the bulbs and replace with new. They can be planted from containers into a shady pocket of a rock garden.

Edelweiss

The best known of all mountain plants must be the edelweiss, which has been commemorated in song, poetry and prose. It has so many myths and legends surrounding it that it has come to be considered by the non-gardener who has never seen it as something which must be of outstanding, perhaps celestial, beauty; many people can be disappointed on seeing a living plant for the first time. The common name, edelweiss, is derived from two German words which in English means 'noble white', a reference to the petal-like bracts which extend beyond the inconspicuous true flowers. These, covered with short hairs, are really grey and seen at their best, when growing on limestone appear no more than greyish white.

In the Latin name *Leontopodium alpinum,* the specific epithet refers to mountains, and the generic name means 'lion's foot'; this, and sometimes 'catspaw', have been used occasionally as alternative common names. To distinguish it from other species of *Leontopodium* and allied genera of similar appearance, edelweiss may be prefixed with 'common'.

L. alpinum is widespread in the European Alps, Pyrenees and Ligurian Apennines and as far east as the Russian Steppes; it can grow at more than 10,000ft (3000m) above sea level. It was introduced into England in 1775 by the Scot, Thomas Blaikie, who was sponsored to collect plants in Switzerland by two London physicians: John Fothergill, who had a private botanic garden at Upton House, West Ham and William Pitcairn, with his botanic garden at Islington. Though Blaikie, the first collector of alpine plants, brought back to England some 400 living specimens, the credit for their introduction is always given to the two doctors. It was during the eighteenth century that it became fashionable for the English to take alpine summer holidays. Being inveterate gardeners they were excited by the alpine meadows with their carpets of flowers and the unusual and unexpected miniature plants seen tucked into crevices or established on screes and moraines. On their return they carried with them many plants for their English gardens and so voracious did this collecting become, that meadows around mountain inns and hospices were soon denuded; the only edelweiss remaining were in inaccessible places. During the nineteenth century, mountaineering developed (along with alpine holidays) as a new sport in which the English excelled. Young men who took up this sport would bring back bunches of edelweiss after their day's climbing, for their girl friends. The recipients of these posies thought that their beloved had risked life and limb on their behalf.

There has never been anyone quite like Reginald Farrer for expressing his dislike of certain plants or for dismissing grandiose claims. In the *English Rock Garden,* he has this to say about the edelweiss:

'To call this plant an alpine, to imagine it rare and precious and difficult of attainment, this is to provoke the meekest into exposure of fraud so impudent and foolish that thereby merits of edelweiss itself are unduly shamed and darkened. It is not an alpine at all; it belongs to the great central European and Asiatic deserts, but, being a profuse seeder, has established itself on every mountain range of the Northern Hemisphere of the Old World. It is not a rarity but is so universally common that you may rely on trampling acres of it on almost any alpine range above the altitude of 5500' . . . Yet every season the misguided go dropping off precipices on which a few stray tufts have seeded down; not knowing that 200' higher, in the short alpine grass, they could be picking basins full of blossoms in half-an-hour's gentle and octogenarian stroll before dinner. So the insane legend still continues fostered by guides who make a practice, in front of hotels of seeming to quest edelweiss along pathless precipices where eye-lash hold is of the slightest . . . Still the reverent enquiry is made in hushed tones "And have you seen the edelweiss?" Still maidens grow misty eyed at the thought of it and after having tramped the Alps from end to end declare that they would die happy if only they could see the edelweiss; an inspiration which proves their pedestrianism never to have progressed beyond the highroads of passes for had they anywhere diverged a hundred yards to the right or left it would have been hard luck indeed had they not found themselves on lawns of their hearts delight'.

Although there were rock gardens during the eighteenth century, these were really arrangements of rocks, often in the form of grottoes. It was in the following century that rock gardens came to be constructed as places on which alpine plants could be grown, and a new garden fashion came into being. The legends that had already begun to surround edelweiss ensured its place on these early rock gardens, but it did not retain the connoisseur's interest for long, for he passed on to more beautiful plants for which a greater skill was required to bring them to bloom and keep them in cultivation.

Edelweiss is an easy plant to grow, and one for every beginner in his first rock garden. It is raised from seed sown thinly on a soil-based seed compost and given the protection of a frame or unheated glasshouse. When the resulting seedlings are big enough to handle, transfer each singly to a small pot using a compost of equal parts of soil, peat and sand. After potting provide some protection, for instance, under a frame, until the plant is established; plant into its permanent position in mid-spring before it is root bound. If it is intended to plant it in a crevice, wash the soil off the root ball under a strong jet of water, and work in the roots together with soil poked in by a narrow stick, ensuring that there are no unfilled spaces and that roots and soils are in close contact. Flowering takes place from late spring to early summer.

Fair Maids of France

Fair maids of France, with its double white flowers, is more common in gardens than the single *Ranunculus aconitifolius*. The species is native to mountain areas of southern Europe, being found in the Alps, Apennines and Pyrenees. The double flowered form seems to have been brought into England by Huguenot refugees who fled from France in 1572, and seems to have preceded the straight species. Gerard was growing both the single and the double forms in his garden at Holborn in 1596; for the double he uses the name 'double white crowfoot', whereas Parkinson calls it 'double mountain crowfoot'. It seems to have acquired the common name of 'Fair maids of France' during the second half of the eighteenth century; the first reference seems to be by Philip Miller in 1753. This is one of a number of plants with double flowers which have been referred to as 'bachelors' buttons' because of their resemblance to these embellishments used to fasten clothes; many small pieces of cloth, held together by a single stitch, were easily attached to clothing by unmarried men. Any of the so-called 'bachelor button' flowers were said to be carried in the pockets of young unmarried men to present to the ladies of their choice.

In the sixteenth and seventeenth centuries all the many kinds of crowfoot seem to have been used for the same ailments. Amongst the virtues listed by Gerard are: leaves of wild or garden forms if applied to the wrists drove away fits resulting from a fever, while a lotion prepared from the leaves would cure the sores and blisters caused by the plague. The most amusing use for crowfoot mentioned by Gerard had been taken from Apuleus: 'If it be hanged in a linnen cloath about the necke of him that is lunaticke at the wain of the moon when the sign shall be in the first degree of Taurus or Scorpio, then he shall forwith be cured'.

Although grown in gardens of the eighteenth century it was always superseded by the more fashionable and flamboyant Asiatic ranunculus, whose cultivation was then at its peak. In 1797 Abercrombie and Mawe in *The Universal Gardener and Botanist* thought highly of it: 'very beautiful and worthy of a place in every garden'. In 1870 William Robinson wrote: 'The flowers are not large, but are so white and neat and pretty and double that they resemble miniature double white Camellias'. The following year, in *Hardy Herbaceous and Alpine Plants,* William Sutherland said that it 'enjoys a very liberal share of the patronage of cottagers and amateurs throughout the country but is not often seen in gardens of larger extent'.

Fair maids of France, when grown in a garden, needs a cool, moist soil and resents warm, dry summers. It can hold its own with any plant in a herbaceous border or island bed. From a loose bunch of dark green, deeply lobed leaves which are triangular in outline rises a much branched stem about 2ft (600mm) in height with fully double clean white flowers up to 3/4in. (18mm) in diameter. The plant is squat enough to need no support when its flowers are produced in spring, and depending on the weather they can last for three weeks. As with all herbaceous border plants, lift every third or fourth year, and after digging over the border and incorporating as much organic matter as is available, divide the plants for replanting at the end of winter. The clump may well be too solid to pull apart, but it can be cut into pieces with a sharp knife or forced apart by two garden forks. To do this, push in the first fork not quite upright so that it crosses the second, which is driven in at the same angle; by pulling the handles together the prongs will force the roots apart. Replant at a distance of 2ft (600mm) apart.

Feverfew

Feverfew is derived from an old French word, *febrifuge,* which means 'to ward off or drive away fever'. Some of its other common names are corruptions or alternative spellings of these two words: 'featherfew', 'fethyfew', 'featherall', 'fedderfew', 'febrifu', 'febrifuga', 'vivrivew' and 'vivvifew'. In addition there are 'hen and chickens', 'flirtwort', 'devil's daisy', 'white wort' and 'St. Peter's wort'; while the double flowered forms are one of a number of plants referred to as 'bachelors' buttons'. Botanists over four centuries have been undecided when classifying this plant, and at various times, it has been included with *Parthenium, Matricaria, Pyrethrum* and *Chrysanthemum,* and may appear in books or seed catalogues under any of these names (different forms can appear in the same catalogue under more than one name. Today its valid name is *Tanacetum parthenium.*

Tanacetum parthenium has been an important medicinal herb for more than two millenia in all the ancient civilisations, so its country of origin is uncertain; it is, however, believed to have come from countries on the Balkan peninsula. Now it is naturalised in most countries in temperate regions of the world. It is a perennial plant which overwinters as a group of short shoots. During spring and summer these elongate and branch and have alternate pinnately lobed, pungent leaves, varying from dark to yellow green. The branches carry bunches of small daisy-like florets with white ray petals and yellow centres.

Introduced into England by the Romans, feverfew was kept alive after their departure in the gardens of monasteries, then the centres of healing. By the sixteenth century it had medicinal uses other than assuaging fevers and agues, for it was an important medicine in curing the ailments of pregnant women. An infusion with honey was taken as a cold cure or to cut phlegm and was used as a gargle for sore throats. Crushed leaves applied as a compress to the pate cured headaches, and leaves pushed into the nostrils and sniffed eased a migraine. Young ladies used a lotion made from it to bathe their faces, to remove freckles, spots and blemishes. Fritters or tansies were made by adding chopped leaves to an egg batter and frying in butter.

In additions to its uses in medicinal ways, feverfew has been grown in gardens for its pretty flowers ever since the introduction of the double flowered form during the sixteenth' century. This was growing in Gerard's garden at Holborn in 1596, and was described by John Parkinson as 'peculiar only to our owne country'. The Dutchman, Crispin van de Passe, in his book *Hortus Floridus* (translated into English in 1614), wrote: 'It abounds in Britain because it appears to be grown there with skill and industry'. At this time the flower was described as being white, and a woodcut in *Hortus Floridus* shows a hemispherical floret which resembles the present day cv 'White Bonnet', whereas the common double in twentieth-century gardens has a flat top and a yellowish centre. Feverfew continued to be grown in gardens of the eighteenth century when there were flowers of varying degrees of doubleness, petals that were flat, rolled or absent, and one kind that was described as having sulphur coloured flowers. With the introduction of the nineteenth century garden fashion of summer bedding, the plant was taken up by seed firms and breeding began. A tall, ungainly plant with single flowers and yellow leaves appeared and although it still exists today it is rare – a good thing for it is a poor plant. Other gold leaf forms were more compact and smaller, down to 12in. (300mm) in height, and today the dwarf forms are less than 6in. (150mm) tall. There is also a group with finely cut golden leaves called 'golden feather'. The ordinary double has been dwarfed too, to produce much branched plants with dark green leaves, less than 8in. (200mm) tall with pom-pom flowers, either yellow or white.

Although feverfew is a perennial, all these forms are treated as annuals. They may be used in annual borders as fillers, island beds, herbaceous or shrub borders, or in pockets on the rock garden. Seed can be sown thinly where the plants are to flower; the seedlings must be thinned, the tall kinds to 12in. (300mm) apart and the dwarf varieties to 6in. (150mm) apart. For bedding, seed is sown in gentle heat with seedlings being pricked off into boxes when large enough to handle, for transplanting into flower beds at the end of spring or after the spring bedding has been cleared. There are two named cvs which are used as permanent plants in a herbaceous border or island bed. These grow to about 18in. (450mm) and have large florets, ¾–1in. (18–25mm) across, with pure white petals. Unlike most plants treated as annuals, there is only a short flowering season. As perennials they are not long lived and can be increased by taking cuttings of non-flowering shoots, although if they are allowed to produce ripe seed, the seedlings will come true. One variety is 'White Bonnet', named by Graham Thomas, and the other, which has dark brown stems, is 'Rowallane' and commemorates the Northern Ireland garden from which it was distributed.

Flame Creeper

Springtime is the most colourful season in a woodland garden with its displays of rhododendrons, primulas and meconopsis all wanting to bloom before the canopy of newly expanding leaves on the deciduous trees shuts out the sunlight. As spring passes into summer a sylvan twilight develops with a paucity of flowers beneath; but it is at this season that the flame creeper begins to provide its floral display. Long, thin, seemingly fragile stems develop annually, in favourable conditions exceeding 6ft (2m), which twine themselves around the supports up which the plant is growing. The first leaves are usually round but soon become deeply lobed. From the upper axils on long stems are produced spurred flowers of five petals, which are like a miniature version of the garden nasturtium, and are of a bright red colour. When the flowers are finished they are replaced by a cluster of three fruits which when ripe are deep blue and contrast with the yellow dying leaves as autumn sets in.

Tropaeolum speciosum was discovered in southern Chile on the island of Chiloe, growing up through the Nothofagus forest, by William Lobb in 1846. He was collecting for the firm of Veitch, and it was at their nursery in Exeter that it was to flower for the first time. It is interesting to read the comment that it did not seem to find the Engish climate to its liking, in *Hortus Veitchii,* a book published by the firm for private circulation in 1906. This plant had arrived in England at a time when rhododendrons were becoming fashionable and extensive plantings were being made in the wetter parts of the country such as Devon and Cornwall and along the west coast of Scotland; as it had come from Chilean rain forests, it too found these parts of the country much to its liking and was soon thriving. In fact it became so common in some Scottish gardens that it acquired an alternative common name in Scottish (flame) creeper. This plant has underground creeping white stems resembling those of bindweed, and when it finds suitable climatic and soil conditions it can be just as much a menace as that notorious British weed.

Sassenach gardeners, not to be denied a plant that did so well in gardens north of the border, were determined to make a success of cultivation. Both William Robinson writing in 1870 and William Sutherland in 1871 comment on the ease in which it grows in Scotland. It is, though, Sutherland who speculates on the reasons why: 'I have also seen it in the south of England refuse to grow in nearly every kind of soil and degree of aspect, even with all conceivable coaxings. This is probably owing to climate. It is very impatient of atmospheric drought, as well as at the roots; and the absence of the long bracing nights and refreshing dews of the north is perhaps the cause of the ill-success of the endeavours I have seen made at cultivating it in the south'. Success can be obtained in south-eastern England but the gardener must be patient. Anywhere that rhododendrons thrive, the flame creeper ought to succeed.

Choose a shady position in a soil well supplied with organic matter, which does not dry out during the summer. Those who do not grow rhododendrons should plant under shrubs at the foot of a north facing wall. Sections of the white underground stems can be planted horizontally a few inches down, in spring, after which the gardener has to wait patiently to see if growth is going to emerge. It may take several years before the plant settles down and begins to grow satisfactorily. Many books recommend planting on the northern side of a yew hedge in a thoroughly moist soil; if it successfully establishes itself, the thin stems climb through the upwards providing a bright splash of colour against the sombre green of the yew.

Seed is one method of increase, but it needs to be fresh and not old or dried. When ripe seed falls to the ground, germination will usually occur in the following spring. If, however, the seed is collected and allowed to dry and sown at a later date, germination rarely takes place. Seed is naturally short lived and requires moist storage for successful germination. Collected seed should be sown immediately it is ripe, after it has been extracted from its fruit and washed; push seeds into small pots of soil so that they are covered and stand outside plunged to their rims, germination should occur in the following spring. Plant into a permanent position when the danger of frost is over but before the plant has become root bound.

Foxglove

Foxglove, *Digitalis purpurea,* is native throughout northern Europe and is now widespread in cool temperate regions of countries in both hemispheres. It is to be found on moist acid soils in ditches, on heathlands, at the edge of woodland and is an early coloniser when woodland or forest has been felled. This biennial produces in its first year a rosette of grey hairy, lance or heart-shaped leaves whose blades gradually taper towards a fairly long leaf stem. In the second year a long flower stalk develops, in a good soil reaching 4ft (1.3m), which is a one-sided spike of pendant elongated bell-shaped flowers, pinkish purple in colour, and spotted; in any colony there will also be white flowers which may or may not be spotted.

In 1542, a German botanist Leonart Fuchs coined the name of *Digitalis* for the genus, whilst the specific epithet *purpurea* is indicative of flower colour. *Digitalis* is from the Latin *digitus* – a finger, and some of the many common names show this same association if the meaning is extended to include 'thimble' or 'glove finger', and allowing for dialect and alternative spellings: 'Our Lady's glove', 'Lady's glove', 'Virgin's glove', 'glove-wort', 'thimbles', 'thimble-flower', 'finger flower', 'fingerwort', 'red finger', 'bloody finger', 'dead-man's finger'. The association of foxglove with the animal has never been easy to understand, unless it refers to the presence of the plants in copses where the fox makes its earth. Two other possible explanations are: that 'fox' is a corruption of 'folk' i.e. good, little or wee folk or fairies; the close resemblance of the plant to a musical instrument of the Middle Ages which consisted of a pole to which bells were fixed. Not only in Britain but in many other countries of Europe there has been an association with fairies and gnomes, as can be seen in the following names: 'fairy-cap', 'fairy fingers', 'fairy petticoats', 'fairy thimbles', 'goblin flower', 'goblin gloves', 'flower-of-the fairies', 'goblins-and-fairies' and 'fairy-hat'. The association with a musical instrument has resulted in: 'foxbell', 'witch's bell', 'dead-man's-bell', 'bell flower' and 'fox chimes'; other common names of unexplained derivation are: 'flop-a-dock', 'lusmore flopadock', 'benweed' and 'foxeyleaves'. 'Snapdragon pops', 'poppies' and 'pop-a-dock' come from children blowing into the flowers until they 'popped'.

Foxglove has long been used medicinally, and at certain periods up to the end of the sixteenth century it seems to have been a panacea for almost all ailments. It is recommended by Gerard as a cure for: ague, fevers, falling sickness, fresh, superating or green wounds, ailments of the liver, spleen and melt; while internally foxgloves were used for cleaning the body of clammy and naughty humours and for cutting phlegm. Yet only 32 years later in 1629 John Parkinson was saying, 'Foxgloves are not used in Physicke by any judicious man that I know'. It was only towards the end of the eighteenth century that foxglove came to be used for heart complaints, and today it is the source of the drug digitalin.

Foxgloves have been tolerated in gardens when they have self sown, but they have never found much favour even though they are showy and easy to grow. They have been tolerated by those people fortunate enough to have an area of woodland, where they would be allowed to colonise at will. For the suburban garden they can bring in a whiff of the countryside by being used as fillers for a herbaceous border, island beds or shrubberies. An interesting experiment is to use them for a late display in spring bedding by using the white flowered form with one of the strong growing onions such as *Allium stipitatum,* or the purple form with *Nectaroscordium siculum.* In the years following the Second World War foxgloves achieved some prominence with the introduction of the Excelsior strain, where flowers were produced all around the stem; in this strain there was an extension of flower colour and the bells were much larger.

Seed is sown in midsummer in a box or nursery bed and pricked out or thinned when large enough to stand 10in. (250mm) apart. Plant out the seedlings into the flower garden in the places where they will flower in early autumn.

Hardy Hibiscus

Hibiscus is a genus of some 200 species of woody plants, mostly confined to the warmer parts of the world. As a common name, hibiscus refers to the tropical *H. rosa-sinensis*, although it has become a general name for most species. Of the few which venture into the cooler parts of the world, the best known is *H. syriacus*; Linnaeus had given it this name in 1753 because he thought that its home was in the Middle East. It has however, been so long cultivated as a garden plant that it is widely distributed far beyond its natural distribution, which may be from Northern India to China. It was possibly introduced into England at the time of the crusades, but it seems more likely to have come from the gardens of the Turkish court in Constantinople via the diplomatic bags of one of the European ambassadors to the Byzantine court, during the middle of the sixteenth century. In 1597, Gerard described it as a new plant; in 1629, Parkinson was growing a white and a purple, to which in 1659 Sir Thomas Hanmer added red and grindeline (a shade of pink). Just over 100 years later, in 1768, Philip Miller listed five colours, while by 1797, Abercrombie and Mawe had added a variegated coloured flower, and in both these lists are recorded plants with silver and golden variegated leaves. The first doubles seem to have appeared early in the nineteenth century for both white and purple double forms are listed in 1829 by Loudon. It was, though, the end of the nineteenth century and the years preceding the First World War before hardy hibiscus reached a peak of popularity.

Until 1753, *Hibiscus syriacus* had been known as *Althaea frutex*, but over the years it has had many common names in English. Perhaps that which has been used longest is 'shrubby mallow' but there have also been: 'tree mallow', 'Venetian mallow', 'Syrian mallow', 'Jew's mallow', 'ketama', 'Syrian ketama', 'shrubby hollyhock' and 'tree hollyhock'. Today it is commonly called 'Syrian hibiscus', but as the specific epithet suggests the wrong country of origin, it is more appropriate that the alternative 'hardy hibiscus' is retained.

In warmer countries than Britain this hardy hibiscus makes a large shrub, even small tree, up to 20ft (6m). There are alternate lobed, almost diamond-shaped, leaves which fall off before winter arrives. Flowers produced in leaf axils on current season's growth are at first cup-shaped but expand until they are almost completely flat. Petals, which usually have a dark base can be white or any shades of pink, red, mauve, purple and almost blue, and there are a few self-colours.

In warm sunny weather, single flowers will last for just one day but on the next day, another flower will have opened. In dull weather, the single flowers may last for a few days, and the doubles will last for several days, irrespective of the weather. Flowering, which can begin in midsummer, will continue into early autumn to be followed by quite large angular bristly upright capsules which split open when ripe to scatter black shiny seed. *H. syriacus* can tolerate much colder winters than those of England as long as the summers are hot and dry so as to ripen the wood thoroughly. The soft wood often fails to ripen properly in cold wet English summers and such wood is prone to winter damage which then becomes infected with coral spot. Although this disease is generally considered a saprophyte, it can also be parasitic and in severe cases can result in the shrub's death.

English gardens are at their peak in late spring after which the floral display declines. This is especially true of shrubs and it seems curious that the hardy hibiscus which comes into flower when the majority of others have ended their display should have fallen so completely out of favour, especially when there is so much variety of colour produced over six to eight weeks.

As Hardy hibiscus flowers on the current season's growth, it should be hard pruned in late spring, just before new growth is about to begin. This hard pruning results in many more larger flowers being produced, often later than on an unpruned bush. In a cold or wet summer a dressing of potash at the rate of one ounce per sq. yd (32 grams per sq. m.) over the root spread will help to reduce winter damage and encourage the bush to withstand disease infection.

If seed is set, this provides a ready means of increase if sown in gentle heat in the following spring. Seedlings take three to four years to bloom, and flower colour will be variable with little chance of it being the same as the parent. Doubles and named cvs should be propagated from cuttings. If there is a frame or glasshouse, cuttings taken from midsummer onwards are not difficult to root. Hardwood cuttings taken after the leaves have fallen can be used by gardeners without protection. Current season's growth cut into lengths of 6–10in. (150–250mm) should be inserted into a sandy soil in a protected part of the open garden so that just their tips are protruding; a fair percentage of these should root.

Heliotrope

The first heliotrope known to gardeners was *Heliotropium europeum* which had the English name of 'turnsole'. Heliotrope is derived from two Greek words meaning 'to turn with the sun', and the English is a corruption of two French words with the same meaning. Botanists from ancient times had mistakenly thought that the flowers followed the sun around the heavens.

Heliotrope is a large genus of which the majority of species are found in South America; the best known, and the plant to which the common name of 'heliotrope' is applied, is *H. peruvianum.* Its date of introduction in European gardens is said to be 1757. Discovered by Joseph de Jussieu in a valley in the Cordillera Centrale north of Lima in Peru, seed was sent back to the Royal Gardens in Paris. Within a few years it must have been in England for in 1768 Philip Miller had already been growing it for a number of years. When it arrived it was as a glasshouse plant and seed which at that time was the main means of increase, was being set regularly. It was a tall, ungainly shrub, untidy in growth and with pallid but highly fragrant bluish flowers. *H. coymbosum,* which arrived in Europe in 1800, was small and compact with larger and more deeply coloured flowers but with little or no fragrance. These two species seem to have been hybridised to produce a race of plants which were to become immensely popular as bedding plants later in the nineteenth century and during the twentieth. In Paxton's *Botanical Magazine* of 1849 is an illustration of a plant called *Heliotropium (peruvianum) voltaireanum,* which is probably the result of this cross. It had all the good characteristics of *H. corymbosum* but with the strong fragrance of *H. peruvianum.* During the latter part of the nineteenth century many forms of heliotrope were produced with differing degrees of vigour, bushiness and flower colour to which cv names were given. These remained immensely popular in gardens up to the Second World War. Probably many were lost when it became increasingly difficult to obtain fuel for glasshouses and non-food plants had to take their chances in unheated structures; certainly, in the post war years few heliotropes remained and even these lost favour. It is surprising that a plant with such a delicious fragrance and long flowering season should have almost disappeared. With a decrease in staff and the increased cost of maintaining heated glasshouses, many plants that had to be propagated vegetatively in the autumn and overwintered in heated structures were neglected. Increasingly after the end of World War II seed houses were producing strains of old, familiar bedding plants that could be treated as annuals; the heliotrope was one of these, but the result was to produce a small-growing race of plants, of uneven habit and virtually scentless. One assumes that growers have concentrated their breeding on *H. corymbosum.* Standard plants have been trained for the two main uses of the heliotrope: as a bedding plant, and as a pot or tub plant for ornamenting a patio or house front to perfume the air for passers-by.

For the fragrant heliotrope it is necessary to propagate by cuttings. Heliotrope is not hardy and will not take any frost, so stock plants have to be kept through the winter in a frost-free house. From stock plants in early spring, if heat is available, cuttings are taken from stock plants, and when rooted they are potted singly. These young plants are kept growing at a steady temperature and planted into the garden as spring passes into summer. When standards are to be trained, cuttings should be rooted as early as possible and kept to a single stem, potted on into larger pots as each fills with roots. Provide the plant with a cane and tie the main stem at regular intervals pinching out side shoots; replace the original cane with one four feet, (1.3m) long when the plant finishes up in its final pot which should be 8in (200mm) in diameter. When the plant reaches 3ft (1m) it can be stopped and allowed to branch. It will take about 18 months to produce a standard plant depending on winter heat. Standard plants can be stood outside as soon as the danger of frost has passed, or they can be planted in amongst bedding as dot plants to provide height; they must be rehoused before the autumn frosts arrive.

Hepatica

Although Linnaeus classified this plant as *Anemone hepatica* in *Species Plantarum* in 1753, not all botanists, even his most ardent followers, accepted the name, preferring instead *Hepatica nobilis,* a name by which it had been known for several hundred years and which today is again the valid name. The present day generic name, and Linnaeus's specific epithet which has become the most usual common name, is derived from a Greek word meaning 'liver'. In the Middle Ages, a plant was thought to cure by signature: if part of a plant resembled an organ of the human body (however fanciful) then it would cure ailments of the organ. Botanists, herbalists and physicians of the fifteenth and sixteenth centuries considered that the leaves resembled the human liver, and so an early common name was 'liverwort'; to separate it from the group of lichens of the same name it was prefaced with the adjective 'noble'. In the *British Physician* of 1664, Robert Turner considered it especially good for young married men who wished to have children.

Double Hollyhocks

Mirabilis Jalapa

Hepatica nobilis (H. triloba) is widespread in mountain woodland of the Northern Hemisphere. Although not native to Britain it must have been an early garden plant in this country, for it is mentioned by John Gardiner in 1440 in his *Feate of Gardening*. In his *Names of Herbes* of 1548, William Turner called it 'Trinitaria', because of the three lobes of the leaf, but he said that there were two plants for which he used this name, the other being hearts-ease *(Viola tricolor)* where the prefix 'tri-' refers to flower colour. Extensive cultivation of the noble liverwort began, following the arrival in England of the Huguenots who had fled from religious persecution in France after the St. Bartholomew's Day Massacre in 1572. These refugees had brought with them their love of plants, and some of the kinds in whose cultivations they were to specialise. They joined together with English enthusiasts to form florists' societies; at this time a florist was an amateur who specialised in the cultivation of many kinds of a single or a few plants. The seventeenth century was to see the birth of the florists' feasts at which flowers were exhibited in competition. During the eighteenth century these were being held in most large towns and cities throughout Britain, and were to be replaced during the following century by the flower shows we know today, where a wide range of garden produce was displayed.

In 1597, Gerard was growing the single red, white and blue and wrote of a double blue which he says 'is yet a stranger in England'; Thomas Johnson however, in his 1633 revision of the *Herbal* says that 'it is now plentifull in England'. In 1629, Parkinson had added to Gerard's list a single and a double purple and, two additional whites, one small with red stamens, and one which was large and ash-coloured in which pink faded to white. In 1659 Sir Thomas Hanmer had singles that were pale and deep blush and a double red. He is one of the few gardeners of the period to mention cultivation:

The plant loves a warme rich mold, and a station under or neere some wall or other place that shelters it from the winds, otherwise they are hardy enough and need not housing, but the Dowble kind never beares faire flowers in smoaky townes but delights in pure ayre. The English name is Liverwort but 'tis commonly called Hepatica by all. The roote is best remov'd or divided about Michaelmas, being in flower soe early in the Spring.

A double white form seems to have been unknown to seventeenth century gardeners, and its breeding seems to have eluded all. Philip Miller in 1768 did not mention it, yet there is a reference to both a single and a double white in the *Universal Gardener and Botanist* by Abercrombie and Mawe in 1796. There is no further mention of a double white until 1904 when, in *Flora and Sylva*, William Robinson wrote, 'Though full flowers in other colours have long been known, if the double white kind ever existed in gardens – a matter of much dispute – it has certainly disappeared until a single wild plant was found by a lad when roaming in the forests of the

Hartz mountains has given us the long desired double white Hepatica'. During the nineteenth century there had been a declining interest in hepatica which William Robinson had tried to stem; in *Alpine Flowers* of 1870 he said, 'There is a cheerfulness and courage about it on a warm sunny border in spring which no other flowers possess'. It would have been expected that with the new garden fashion of rock gardens, the hepatica would have been an ideal plant for an alpine enthusiast. Perhaps it was the meagre praise afforded it by the arch-priest of rock gardeners, Reginald Farrer, which discouraged disciples of this new fashion from introducing it into their gardens. Nevertheless, today it is the rock gardeners who are growing this plant in a shady part of their rock or peat garden, for it provides a succession of blooms throughout late winter and early spring. It is the single blue, occasionally the white, which is most often seen; the doubles seem to be extremely rare.

Seed of the singles is set in most years; this is the easiest method of raising young plants and it should be sown outside as soon as it is ripe, with germination occurring in the following spring. Doubles are best divided in late summer, but they increase so slowly that division should take place of large clumps only and these should not be broken up into too many pieces. While hepatica is indifferent to soil type, it does need plenty of organic matter and a soil which does not dry out in summer.

Holly

Christmas and its preparations dominate December. It is now the only annual festival for which the house is decorated. In northern Europe there are few flowering plants growing in the garden at this season which can be used for decoration so, their place is taken by cut branches of evergreens: pine, juniper, yew and box but above all, holly, which, with its red berries, is especially attractive at this season.

The use of holly to decorate the home at this time of the year predates Christianity. It was used by druids in winter ceremonies and by the Romans in their festival of saturnalia which was celebrated at the time of the winter solstice. Celebrations for this festival were taken over by the early Christians when they came to commemorate the birth of Christ. It was said to be bad luck to use holly to decorate the home before the eve of Christmas; no doubt to ensure that it was to celebrate a Christian festival and not a pagan rite. At one time it was removed on the eve of Candlemas (2nd February) but tradition now removes it on Twelfth Night. Many myths and legends are associated with holly: it has been considered to give protection against witches and mischievous goblins, and when planted near a house it was said to provide protection against being struck by lightning. The prickly kind of holly used to be described as 'male', and the smooth kind as 'female'; if the former thrived in a garden and/or was taken into the house then the husband would be master, if the latter then it would be the wife. Male and female hollies have been used in various ceremonies to enable young men and maidens to know their future spouse.

Ilex aquifolium is widespread from China westward right through Europe and into Britain. Although more often a shrub, it can make a tree up to 80ft (25m). The trees are long lived, and although there are many exaggerations of age, there are a number of well documented cases in England of trees over 300 years old; two trees mentioned by Pliny, however, of 800 and 1200 years, raise doubts. Holly passes through two stages of growth: juvenile, when the leaf margins are undulate and spiny, and adult, when leaves are flat and their margins smooth. The alternate evergreen leaves show great diversity in size, form and colour even on the same tree. In late spring clusters of small white fragrant flowers are produced in the axils of previous seasons' growth, which on any one tree are either male or female (very rarely both). It is necessary to have trees of both sexes in close proximity to get a crop of berries. Once it was nursery practice to graft a male branch onto a female holly bush to ensure a regular crop of berries, but this has been discontinued; no doubt a nurseryman prefers to sell two plants rather than one. Gardeners beware! Some cultivar names can be misleading: both Golden Queen and Silver Queen are males. Bright red is the colour expected of holly berries; it is usually the uncommon which attracts gardeners, yet yellow berried hollies have never been popular. John Evelyn mentions a holly with white berries which may be the same as the Herefordshire White, listed by Philip Miller; this seems to have been lost from gardens since then, for the last mention of it was by John C. Loudon in the *Gardeners' Magazine* in 1843.

Good crops of berries are not an indication of a severe winter, but rather that at flowering the weather had been fine and warm, allowing good pollination. A gardener may feel very satisfied when he sees his holly laden with berries a few weeks before Christmas, but dismayed when he goes to cut branches for the house only to find that birds have stripped the holly of its fruits. Some trees suffer this fate every year, and yet on others close by, berries are untouched. It is probably that the sugar content in berries differs from tree to tree and birds take only those which they find palatable. Trees can be found that carry two or three years' berries.

The present generic name of *Ilex* formerly referred to an evergreen oak, *Quercus ilex,* and is used still as a common name for this tree. Before 1753, the botanical name had been *aquifolium,* which has now become the specific epithet. Local names and those in use in former times include: 'acutifolium', 'agrifolium'; holm', 'hulme', 'hulver', 'killin', 'Christ thorn', 'Christmas', 'prickbush', 'prick-hollin' and 'hollin'; 'holy' is also said to have been used, because branches were used to decorate churches for the most joyous of Christian festivals, but it is more likely that this was just an alternative way of spelling 'holly'. Until the nineteenth century, spelling was never precise and it was not uncommon to see a word spelt in more than one way even on the same page.

It would seem that holly was brought into gardens during the seventeenth century. Gerard describes it as a wild plant, Parkinson omits it from his *Paradisus* although it is in his *Theatrum Botanicum.* In *The Garden Book* of Sir Thomas Hanmer, he has written:

Though it is soe common that it growes voluntarily in woods and hedges, yet being it is a greene that may bee kept with cutting well in any forme and beautifull both in the leaves and berrys. I added it to the rest. I have seene a walke of these trees cut into Pyramides, and growing soe very high with leaves from the ground to the top, that it hath beene a very grateful sight. There is a fine variegated kind of holly, the leaves being stript with yellow and greene, which is all the differences I know of this tree'.

In the 1706 edition of *Sylva,* John Evelyn mentions six or seven kinds; at his garden at Sayes Court he had a holly hedge of which he was immensely proud. 'Is there under Heaven a more glorious and refreshing Object of the Kind, than an impregnable Hedge of about Four hundred foot in Length, nine Foot high, and five in Diameter'. This hedge was destroyed by the antics of The Czar of Russia to whom Evelyn leased Sayes Court in 1698: the Czar had his courtiers push him in a wheelbarrow into and through the hedge and completely spoiled it. In Evelyn's diary for 9th June 1698 he wrote 'I went to Deptford to see how miserably the Czar had left my house after 3 months making it his Court. I got Sir Christopher Wren, the Kings surveyor, and Mr (George) London his gardener, to go and estimate the repairs, for which they allowed £150 in their report to the Lords of the Treasury'.

It was, however, in the eighteenth century that hollies really began to gain favour: in 1768, Philip Miller mentioned 16 kinds, and Mawe and Abercrombie in 1797 had 22. Holly reached its peak in the nineteenth: in 1863 William Paul wrote of 73 kinds, 11 years later Thomas Moore described 151. By 1908, though, Dallimore had only 100 varieties and five years later Henry and Elwes listed fewer than 40 (these may be only botanical forms rather than cvs); in the eighth edition of Bean, published in 1973, the number just exceeds 50, although it is doubtful if any nursery today would offer even half of this number.

Over the centuries there have been many uses for holly. In medicine, leaves from which the spines had been removed, were dried, powdered and added to wine and used to cure by signature stitch and pricking pains in the side. The chewing of ripe berries eased colic, while drinking ale in which berries had been boiled provided a cure for gallstones or kidney stones. For centuries a most efficient bird-lime was prepared from holly branches. The timber is easy to cut when green but is so hard when seasoned that cutting implements are quickly blunted. In *Sylva* John Evelyn wrote:

The Timber of the Holly (besides that it is the whitest of all hard Woods and therefore used by the Inlayer, especially under thin Plates of Ivory to render them more conspicuous) is for all sturdy uses; the Millwright, Turner and Engraver prefer it to all other, it makes the best Handles and Stocks for Tools, Flails, Riding-rods the best, and Carters Whips; Bowles, Chivers, and Pins for Blocks; Also it excels for Door-bars and Bolts; and as of the Elm, so of this especially they made even Hinges and Hooks to serve instead of Iron, sinking in the Water like it . . .

Holly is tolerant of a wide range of soils, whether acid or alkaline, but it dislikes one which is thin and dry, nor will it tolerate waterlogging. It can be planted near the sea for it is unharmed by salt spray. Even though its appearance can be marred by atmospheric pollution it is well able to grow in the most industrialised of towns and cities.

In a garden today holly can be used as a specimen tree, as a constituent of a shrub border, or for a topiary subject, although it tends to be mostly used for making hedges which are impenetrable and stock proof. When preparing the ground for a hedge, double dig a trench at least a yard (metre) wide incorporating as much organic matter into the lower spit as is available. Allow the soil to settle and thoroughly tread before planting a single line of plants at 3ft (1m) spacing at the beginning of spring. Wherever hollies are to be planted, it is better to buy two or three year old bushes which are not only cheaper but will establish more quickly than larger and older ones. After the bushes have been planted, apply a mulch to a 3ft (1m) strip on either side of the hedge, and continue to do this in the early years following planting; in subsequent years replace the mulch with a dressing of a general fertiliser to the same width of strip at the rate of 2oz per yard (68 grams per metre) run. Trimming of the hedge should be done once in midsummer after the new growth is complete.

Large quantities of holly can be raised from seed, although germination tends to be erratic and delayed. After gathering fully ripe fruit, fill a container provided with drainage with alternate layers of berries and a peat/sand mixture; cover with wire netting as a protection against vermin and plunge in the open garden. Seed is removed and sown in nursery rows at the end of a second winter. Named cvs are propagated from cuttings taken in late autumn, or winter, prepared in the normal way from current season's growth with an inch-long thin sliver of bark removed from the base which is dipped into a rooting hormone for hard-wood cuttings. Although the quickest and best rooting is obtained when there is bottom heat, cuttings inserted into a peat/sand mixture in an unheated glasshouse or frame will eventually produce roots.

Hollyhock

Hollyhock is a tall stately perennial plant that is used today in gardens in herbaceous borders, large island beds or in groups amongst shrubs. It has a long history, being known to most of the early civilisations around the Mediterranean. Many books suggest that it grows wild in China, but its exact country of origin is uncertain; it is, however, more likely to be from Near East rather than the Far East. It may have been introduced into England by the Romans, without establishing itself. Its common name is a corruption of 'holy hoc': *hoc* is a Saxon word for 'mallow' while the religious connotation of 'holy' suggests it to be a plant brought back home by the crusaders from countries over which they fought the Turks. It was known in English gardens of the sixteenth century, and became widely grown in the following century. Sir Thomas Hanmer was growing plants with single and double flowers with colours ranging from white, pink, blush, carnation, scarlet, blood red, and crimson to almost black. He also mentions a yellow, a colour which though not found in *Althaea rosea,* occurs in a closely related species *A. ficifolia,* so hybridisation must have occurred; Sir Thomas mentions too a double yellow which had come from the garden of the Duc d'Orleans. In his *Garden Book* of 1659 we read: 'The plant is fittest for courts and spatious gardens, being soe great and stately'.

Dioscorides writing in *Materia Medica c.* 500 AD had said that hollyhock was bad for the stomach and good for the belly, stalks being preferable for the entrails and the bladder. English herbalists of the sixteenth and seventeenth centuries used hollyhock in the same way as they did other kinds of mallow. A poultice made from leaves, sometimes with bean or barley flowers, was used to ease the pain and reduce swellings in tumours and inflammations and was more effective when applied warm;

one of green leaves with saltpetre was used to remove prickles, thorns and spines. Flowers, providing a dye, when boiled in wine and water to which had been added some honey, was used as a gargle. Chopped young leaves were added to salads, although John Evelyn considered them better when added to the pot in which stews and broths were being prepared.

Hollyhocks continued to be fashionable during the eighteenth century but it was during the nineteenth that they reached a peak. Ever-increasing numbers of seedlings were being raised by nurserymen in their search for novelty in flower form and colour. The best of these were propagated by cuttings and it is curious to read that for a plant which is not difficult to propagate by this means it was also propagated by saddle grafts. Suburbia had begun to develop after the Industrial Revolution and small terraced houses were being built to provide accommodation for country-folk who were flocking into towns and cities. The gardens of suburbia were smaller than those owned by the gentry and the terrace gardens were tiny. Nurseries now found that the gentry no longer made up the largest proportion of their clientele, so they were providing plants more suitable for much smaller gardens; breeding was producing hollyhocks of lesser stature. As the nineteenth century declined so did the fashion for growing hollyhocks, coinciding with the arrival of a rust disease. This disease showed itself as reddish pustules on the undersurface of the leaf, producing unsightly yellowing on the upper surface and a loss of vigour. By the beginning of the Second World War, the cultivation of hollyhocks had almost ceased. In the years which followed, plant breeders did what they could to increase the demand for hollyhocks by attempting to raise rust-resistant strains, but this met with limited success, for either the disease became more virulent or seedlings lost their resistance. By 1960 the hollyhock was once again in danger of disappearing from gardens, but there was a change in methods of cultivation, with plants being treated as annuals or biennials. After flowering the plants were removed and burnt, so preventing a carry-over of the disease to the next season. Whether because the disease began to lose its virulence or this alternative method of cultivation proved the answer, hollyhocks are once again being grown in gardens.

Wherever hollyhocks are to be grown, remember that they need plenty of room. Seed can be space sown in early spring where plants are to flower; they may or may not flower in the first season, depending on the summer. Guaranteed or earlier flowering can be assured by sowing seeds in containers under glass at the end of the winter to be planted into the garden in mid – late spring. In gardens in an area which has long, warm summers, ripe seed will be produced which may self sow, but which the gardener can, if he wishes, collect for his own use. Always select seed from the best colour forms and rogue out inferior plants.

Honesty

In Gerard's *Herbal* we read 'among our women it is called honestie', and while this is the first recorded time that this name was used, it was not to become general until the nineteenth century, a romantic age when a language of flowers developed for use by young ladies and the love-lorn. Its association with truth may have arisen when it was thought to thrive only in the garden of an honest man.

It has the botanical name of *Lunaria annua (L. biennis)*; the generic name was given to the plant because of the shape of the fruits, which resemble the full moon, *luna* in Latin. This lunar likeness has produced a number of English names: 'moons', 'moonwort', 'full moon', 'silver moon' and 'lunaria'; there is also a fern *Botrychum lunaria* which has been called both 'moonwort' and 'lunaria' because of the shape of the pinnae. The shape of the siliqua to which the seeds are attached and which remains after they have been distributed were thought by countryfolk to resemble coins, hence the name 'money', 'moneywort', 'money-plant', 'money-flower', 'money-in-both-pockets', 'pennies', 'silver-penny', 'silver-monies', 'silver-shilling', 'shilling flower', 'pennywort' and 'penny-flower'. From the shining surface of the siliqua come 'satin-flower', 'white-satin-flower', 'silks-and-satins', 'silken-flower', and 'paper flower'; other names are: 'bolbanac', 'prick-songwort' and 'lunacy', which may be a misspelling of 'lunarie' or an indication that honesty will cure mental disorders. A French word for this plant is *lunette* meaning 'spectacles', a translation which has been used by English folk.

In the dark ages honesty was much used by witches and warlocks in spells, incantation, charms, enchantment and bewitchments and it was said to have the power to put monsters to flight. No herbal remedies using it are recorded, but its young leaves, chopped finely, were added to salads or to pottage before serving.

Today it is grown in gardens for its attractive shining papery siliqua, which is much used in dried flower arrangements. Their use in winter may not be to everyones taste, but they are preferrable to arrangements of plastic flowers. Plants to provide them are grown in the corner of the vegetable garden or in a place set aside for cut flowers. Honesty is not gathered until after the seed have become detached from siliqua. For a plant to produce seed, it has first to flower, and it is surprising how little attention is paid to honesty when it is in flower. The flowers are profusely produced and last for two to three weeks; they are available in the usual pink forms, and also in white, purple and red. It can make an interesting ground cover plant for spring bedding if planted with a tall growing bulb such as *Camassia leichtlinii* or *C. cuisickii*, or a flowering onion such as *Allium stipitatum*. Its flowers last for too short a time to be used elsewhere in the garden.

Honesty is a biennial and seed is sown outside in late summer, either directly where it is to flower or in a nursery bed for transplanting. The large seed is not difficult to handle and can be space sown. There is a virus disease which causes colour breaking in the mauve, pink or red flowers although it is unnoticed in the white; this disease is spread by aphis and the developing seedlings should be sprayed at regular intervals to keep these pests at bay. In a cottage-type garden where the contents are informal, seedlings will appear without sowing every year and these should be thinned rigorously otherwise they will be in danger of swamping more desirable subjects.

Honeysuckle

As a common name, 'honeysuckle' has come to be used for all species of *Lonicera* and yet it was originally intended for the deciduous *Lonicera periclymenum*. The generic name commemorates the botanist Adam Lonitzer (1528–86) who wrote a herbal which went to several editions and was as popular in Germany as Gerard's *Herbal* was in England. *Periclymenum*, meaning to roll or twine around, is the Greek name for the plant, but it was used also as a generic name by botanists and herbalists until Linnaeus introduced his binomial systems in *Species Plantarum* (1753) on which modern plant classification is based. Some of its common names are: 'honeysuckle', 'suckles', 'sweet suckle', 'suckle-busk', 'suck-lings', 'bind', 'bindwood', 'woodbind', 'woodbine', 'woodwind', 'honey-bind' and 'fairy-trumpets'; two interesting common names of obviously recent times are: 'gramophones' and 'gramophone horns'. The flowers do produce quantities of nectar as its name might indicate, but some references suggest that it takes its name from the honey-dew secreted by aphis, which often infests growing shoots and flower buds. 'Bine' is a dialect word for a climbing lax stem or it might be a corruption or alternative spelling of 'bind' meaning to fasten or attach to. Woodbine as older readers will know was a brand name for a cheap cigarette; could it be that the manufacturers thought they could gull the buying public into thinking that the fragrance of the tobacco or its smoke would evoke the scents of the countryside? William Turner in 1548 gives an alternative name for honeysuckle of *Chevres feuille* which he says is the name used in France; the translation is 'goat's leaf', a name sometimes used in England. In patois, *chevre feuille* became *cherfeu,* which, when translated into English, became 'dear fire' or 'dear flame'; and so, in the language of flowers, honeysuckle came to be a sign of ardent or endearing love.

In the Middle Ages, honeysuckle was planted near the house to provide protection against witches and wizards. Farmers in Scotland would plant it by the doors to their byres to ensure that their animals were safe from spells cast upon them. Bunches or garlands of honeysuckle were used to adorn cows to provide protection on May Day when the malice of witches and warlocks was most to be feared. On the other hand the good white witches were able to cure many ailments by urging their 'customers' through a honeysuckle archway that they had trained in the woods. It had more practical uses in medicine: a decoction of leaves and flowers with figs and liquorice cured colds in the head or on the chest and cleared phlegm from the nasal passages. Dried leaves smoked with tobacco, or used in its stead, provided a cure for asthma. An infusion of leaves drunk nightly by men or women acted as a contraceptive, but herbalists warned against exceeding 30 days continuously otherwise the drinker would become barren. When an infusion was made from the flowers, it was used by women for bathing the face to remove bruises, blemishes, freckles and sunburn and could be used as a mouthwash or gargle for sore throats, mouth sores and bad breath. Fresh flowers were added to salads in early summer or they could be candied for use at other seasons. A conserve of the flowers was eaten in the same way as jam and was used to disguise the foul taste of children's medicine.

In Tudor and Stuart times, honeysuckle was used to train over arbours and for making pleached bowers; Hanoverian gardeners trained it into standards. Parkinson in his *Paradisus* wrote: 'The honeysuckle that groweth wilde in every hedge although it be very sweete, yet doe I not bring into my garden but let it rest in his owne place to serve their senses that travel by it, or have no gardens'.

Widespread all over Europe, *Lonicera periclymenum* is common in Britain in thin deciduous woodland, especially on regrowth following felling, in copses and in hedgerows. It is a climbing plant that holds itself up by twining around a portion of a woody plant for support, preferring strong, upright thin stems. These twining stems can exert so much pressure on other living stems that there is a strangling effect. When walking sticks were *de rigeur* for men, it was fashionable when walking in the countryside to use a stick that had a deeply indented spiral, caused by the honeysuckle. In the lower parts of the stem, opposite leaves are oval or oblong, but in the upper portions the stem is encircled by round leaves. The cluster of flowers on the terminal portion of the shoots consists of long curving tubes with wide reflexing mouths, which are pale yellow sometimes marked with red, and have a delicious fragrance more noticeable during the early morning, evening and at night; following the flowers a cluster of small, soft, reddish berries develops.

Many gardeners of the seventeenth century, as well as those in later years, came to prefer forms from Holland or Germany which are tidier plants with stronger coloured flowers. Still available today, these are the Dutch honeysuckle (*L. periclymenum* 'Belgica') and the red German Honeysuckle (*L. periclymenum* 'Serotina'). In the twentieth century *L. periclymenum* seems to have been discarded in favour of other honeysuckles which have larger and more colourful flowers but are so often without scent. This is unexpected when fragrance in flowers is so prized and conjures up memories of childhood in the summer gardens of grandparents.

There is much to be said for following John Parkinson's advice to leave the honeysuckle in the hedgerow. It does not always grow successfully in gardens, and in many it is prone to annual infestations by greenfly or blackfly, which not only disfigures young shoots but can be so severe that flowering does not take place. The Dutch and German honeysuckles are not only easier to grow, but are tidier and less prone to infestation. If the gardener does decide to introduce the common honeysuckle into the garden he should ensure that there is a strong trellis up which it can grow, for with age the stems can become large, substantianal and heavy. It can be trained to grow through or over an old tree where its strangling habits will cause no problems. Plant into a carefully prepared hole, some distance from the trunk, and provide string or brushwood to take stems up into the branches. If the tree canopy is dense the ground beneath may be dry, and watering is advisable throughout the summer until the young plant has become established. Cuttings of young non-flowering shoots taken in late summer are not difficult to root.

Ivy-leafed Cyclamen

Cyclamen is a genus of perhaps 18 species which occur in countries around the Mediterranean, in Europe, Asia Minor and in North Africa. These tuberous plants are dormant in the hot, dry summers of these countries, and begin leaf growth with the arrival of autumn rains. Flowers may be produced before the leaves, or appear with the leaves during winter or spring. Many species are unreliable outdoors where winters are cold, and in those countries which have frost-free winters, but wet summers, flowering can be sparse. In Britain most species are pot-grown in frames or glasshouses where protection can be afforded from the cold of the winter and the wetness in summer. Even when not in active growth, these tubers benefit from the higher temperatures experienced under glass; this induces better flowering. The florists' cyclamen, which has been bred from *C. persicum,* is well-known even to non gardeners as house plants, but all species are fashionable amongst rock garden enthusiasts and are frequently seen at their shows. Amongst the few varieties hardy enough for outdoor cultivation and to tolerate cool, often wet British summers and still flower well, is the ivy-leafed cyclamen (*C. hederifolium*).

The word 'cyclamen' is derived from the Greek word *cyclos*, meaning 'a circle', and refers to the way in which the flower stem elongates after fertilisation and then coils to draw the developing seed pod down to ground level; the specific epithet means 'with a leaf like ivy'. Although cyclamen is occasionally called 'sowbread' because in its native countries pigs dig up tubers for food, the generic name is, and has been for some 300 years, used as a common name for all species.

The ivy-leafed cyclamen, the most widespread species in the genus, is found in Italy, Greece, Yugoslavia and Turkey. Tubers, which can vary in depth in the soil from being just covered to many inches/mm deep. Tubers are more or less round in outline and oval in cross-section, dark brown, almost black on the outside and with white flesh. Roots are produced from the top of the tuber or from around its edges unlike all other species where they come from the undersurface. The flowers, which are produced in late summer and can continue to appear for a period of six or more weeks, have the typical swept-up petals of rose; purplish pink or with a reddish purple blotch at the auriculed base, but there is also a pure white form. Some cyclamen flowers have a fragrance. Leaves do not appear until the flowers are fading and grow horizontally beneath the soil surface before they emerge at some distance from the tuber. They are extremely variable and although most often resembling an ivy leaf with pointed lobes, they can be narrow or almost triangular.

Just as the shape is variable so is the patterning on the leaf; it may be no more than a silver line or silver blotches, bands and zones, but there are some plants in which the entire leaf is silver. Leaves can have a beauty that provides an added interest after the flowers have faded, for they last until late spring, when they will eventually turn yellow and die away. The spherical fruits which have been developing at ground level may not be fully mature when the leaves die down. When they are ripe these burst to disclose closely packed orange seeds with a sticky covering, attractive to ants, which are responsible for seed distribution. New plants are easily raised from this seed which, when fresh, germinates relatively quickly (4–6 weeks). Old seed takes many weeks, even months, to germinate, and then erratically; the process can be speeded up by soaking old seed in cold water for 24 hours before sowing. Seed, the only reliable method of propagation, will produce seedlings mostly identical with the parent.

The ivy-leafed cyclamen was introduced into English gardens 400 years ago, probably from the Naples area of Italy, for an alternative botanical name has been *C. neapolitanum*. Although always prized for its beautiful flowers, as with all other plants in the seventeenth century it had to have more practical uses too: a distillation of the roots was used as a gargle or mouth wash to cure toothache; sniffed up the nose it cured nose-bleed and eased migraine; when poured into the ears it eased or cured deafness; it lessened the discomfort of piles and it cured colic and jaundice. Gerard warned of its danger to pregnant women, and wrote that areas of the garden in which cyclamen were growing should be fenced off for if they were walked over, a miscarriage would result. This cyclamen seems to have been grown by all the well-known gardeners of the seventeenth century, and Philip Miller in 1768 was saying that it 'will thrive in the open air in England and is never killed by the frost'. One hundred years later, William Robinson wrote: 'This species is so perfectly hardy as to make it desirable not only for the rock garden but also for the open border'. It even pleased Reginald Farrer, who tended to denigrate easily grown plants:' The plant is of delicate beauty, and extreme freedom of flowering; making solid clumps of soft flesh colour or carmine in an open sunny gravel path, no less than thriving as heartily if not with such condensed ferocity of floriferousness in places not so inhumane'.

While it has always been a plant for rock gardeners, it has also been a species for the beginner who, finding it easy to cultivate, has passed on to other more demanding species of this attractive genus. It is seen at its best, though, when naturalised in a woodland garden where shade is not too dense, and where it can spread and colonise so that at flowering time there is a pink haze from the countless blooms. The ivy-leafed cyclamen can be planted in groups amongst shrubs or at the front of herbaceous borders or island beds; do mark the position so that when dormant they are not disturbed by routine cultivation. It is indifferent to soil, whether acid or alkaline, as long as it contains plenty of organic matter in the form of leaf mould or peat. When introducing ivy-leafed cyclamen into your garden, use pot-grown plants; do not be tempted by dry tubers often offered for sale in supermarkets. These may seem a bargain when the tubers are so large, but if they have no roots they are difficult to establish and many will die. Plant them in groups from pots in the spring, while in active growth, with the crown just below the surface.

If your cyclamen are to be grown in containers, use a well drained soil based compost containing organic matter and lime. Grow one tuber to a 5in. (125mm) pot or three or five tubers to a 8 or 10in. (200–250mm) pan or shallow pot; pot-grown cyclamen should have their crowns exposed. Water regularly when in active growth, but by late spring reduce the water; do not dry off completely, however, keeping the compost always just moist. When they are dormant expose fully to sun in the warmest part of the garden to ensure free and regular flowering.

Jew's Mallow

This shrub, a native of China, was introduced into Japan more than a thousand years ago, and escaping from cultivation it became widespread on the island of Honshu, where the double flowered form seems more common than the single. Japan was closed for several centuries to Europeans with the exception of the Dutch, who were allowed a trading post on the island of Deshima in Nagasaki Bay. This post was under the control of the Dutch East India Company, and while its servants were allowed a restricted movement on the mainland, it was always under guard. Amongst the appointments made to the post over a period of 150 years, there were three physicans who were also botanists: Kaempfer, Thunberg and Siebold. The German, Englebert Kaempfer, was the first European to see this plant, possibly in a garden at the end of the seventeenth century, it was not until almost a century later, though, that it was described in *Flora Japonica* by the Swedish botanist, Carl Thunberg, published in Europe in 1784. The plant on which his description was based had double flowers, and having no reproductive organs it was wrongly classified as *Corchorus japonicus* of the *Tiliaceae* family, to which the lindens belong. Another species of *Corchorus, C. olitorius,* an Indian plant from which the fibre jute has been extracted, had been known in Europe since the early years of the seventeenth century. At that period it was being grown in gardens as a salad plant and John Parkinson had referred to it in *Theatrum Botanicum* as Jews Mallow. When Linnaeus, also a Swede, had classified all the then known plants, he had put this plant into the rose family, considering it to be a kind of bramble under the name of *Rubus japonicus*. It was a French botanist Alphonse de Candolle, who recognised that it was unrelated to any other plant in the rose family and created for it a new genus, calling it

Kerria japonica. The generic name commemorates William Kerr who had first introduced the living plant into England. Kerr had been chosen by Sir Joseph Banks to go to China when it was opened up to Europeans at the beginning of the nineteenth century, and *K. japonica* was one of the plants which he sent back to the Royal Botanic Gardens at Kew in 1805. It was probably the Thunberg specimen on which de Candolle based his description, so *K. japonica* refers to the double flowered form. John Reeves sent back the single flowered form to the Horticultural Society in 1835, and this became *K. japonica simplex.* 'Jew's Mallow', which was wrongly attributed, is still more frequently used, although the genus is also a frequent common name. The only other which is occasionally seen is 'Japanese rose' but this has also been applied to some forms of *Camellia japonica.*

In the early years following its introduction, *K. japonica* was grown as a glasshouse plant, but once its hardiness was realised, it was soon being grown in gardens. By 1838, J. C. Loudon was saying that it was so common as to be found in the gardens of labourers' cottages. Besides the single and double flowered forms, the only others known in English gardens are singles with variegated foliage, either white or yellow. In Japan there seem to be one or two more with flowers which have different degrees of doubleness or which are paler yellow.

The double form is much the better, having greater vigour, larger flowers and a longer flowering season, while the weaker single with quite small flowers tends to have one season of flowering, and rarely, small uninteresting nut-like fruits sheathed by the persistent calyx. A shrub with a suckering habit, it produces upright bright green slender stems up to 6ft (2m) tall which have lance-shaped toothed leaves up to 4in. (100mm) long. Flowers resembling small double roses are most numerous in spring on bare shoots, but they continue sporadically throughout the summer, although the leaves can obscure them. In autumn, leaves turn a pale yellow before they fall, and the bare bright green stems provide an interesting winter display.

K. japonica is an easy plant for a shrub border or a wild garden, and is indifferent to soil as long as it is well drained; it will perform satisfactorily even on the poorest soil. Although it can be left to its own devices some pruning is beneficial to thin crowded shoots to remove the oldest and weakest stems and to prevent it encroaching on its neighbours. Because flowers are produced on previous season's growth, annual pruning can be carried out when all but one-year-old stems are removed. Propagation can be by cuttings taken from non-flowering growth in late summer, under protection. It is, though, easier to lift the plant in winter, pull apart, cut back to 12in. (150mm) and replant each rooted piece.

Judas Tree

Legend has it that it was on this tree that Judas hanged himself after his betrayal of Christ, but there are many other trees to which this legend is also attached. The old name was *arbor judae,* which can be translated as 'the tree of Judaea' or even 'Jewish tree', so the common name may be indicative of country of origin. *Cercis siliquastrum* (its botanic name) is common in countries at the eastern end of the Mediterranean, and extends into Asia Minor. It is not known when it first came into England but there must have been many introductions. Travellers in the Holy Land would probably have been entranced by the beauty of this tree when in bloom and would have brought back seed to England. There is a mention by William Turner in 1548 of a tree called *siliqua,* which modern botanists suggest is the Judas Tree, but this must be incorrect for he goes on to say that 'it may be called in English, Carobe tree and the fruits Carobe or Carobbeane'; this must refer to *Ceratonia siliqua,* which today is commonly called the carob. There is no doubt that it was being grown in Gerard's garden at Holborn in 1597, for there is a very clear woodcut in his *Herbal.* It appears in all the lists of plants being grown by the famous gardeners of the seventeeth century (Parkinson, Coys, Tradescant, Rea and Sir Thomas Hanmer), and was offered for sale in the catalogue of William Lucas in 1677. At this period, prices rarely appeared with plants, but in 1775 in the catalogue of John and George Telford of York a Judas tree cost one shilling which probably corresponds to £10 today. During the seventeenth century, white flowers were known, as well as the usual purplish pink; in the next century Miller added flesh colour to the list of colours, and in 1944 a branch with deep reddish purple flowers was exhibited at the Royal Horticultural Society. Trees with double flowers and leaves variegated with yellow or white have also been recorded.

Although always grown for the beauty of its flowers, the Judas tree also had other uses. John Evelyn considered it as a salad plant and wrote in his *Acetaria, a discourse on Sallets* of 1699: 'Judas Tree – *Arbor judae:* its pretty light coloured Papilionaceous Flowers have a very grateful acidity and thereby gain'd Admittance amongst our Acetaria'. Flowers in springtime were added fresh to salads and were sometimes candied for use at other seasons; a pickle of the flowers in wine vinegar was much enjoyed. At this period pickles were stored in pottery galley pots which excluded light; if today a pickle of Judas flowers is kept in glass jars exposed to light, the flower colour changes to an unappetising dirty grey or brown.

The wood of the Judas tree is hard and beautifully grained with black and green veining and has been used in cabinet work and for inlaying. The tree can reach a great age and is slow growing, rarely exceeding 20ft (6m) although trees two or more centuries old can be double this height., It does not always make a tree and can be shrublike with a number of main stems. Even if it does develop a single trunk, this can produce a mass of twiggy growth along the bole and limbs with suckers arising from the roots at some distance from the tree. In 1659 Sir Thomas Hanmer wrote that when these were dug up with some root they afforded a method of propagation. Flowering of a suitably placed tree often begins at an early age and this, together with its slow growth, makes it well suited to a small suburban garden. Flowers are produced on spurs which can be so compressed as to be scarcely discernable, suggesting that flowering is taking place directly from the trunk or limbs. Purplish pink flowers appear on naked branches in early spring, although when flowering is delayed, as after a late winter or during a cold spring, leaves and flowers develop together so spoiling the floral effect. Leaves, which normally emerge after flowering, are of a pale bluish green and may be round or kidney-shaped. With the arrival of autumn after a warm and sunny summer, these turn yellow, even gold, before they fall. Even in winter the tree can attract attention with its hanging seed pods and gnarled, often leaning, appearance.

The Judas tree needs a light, well drained soil which can be either acid or alkaline, and a sunny position protected from wind and not subject to late spring frosts. It is best planted in isolation, making an excellent specimen tree for the centre of a lawn. While bare rooted seedlings one or two years old establish most easily, older and larger plants from containers do not present any difficulties as long as they are not root bound. Some pruning is beneficial, especially in the early years to train a trunk and provide a well spaced framework of branches. At all times keep the trunk clean of twiggy growth and remove thin, weak, crowded and crossing shoots in the crown. Pruning should be carried out following flowering, but unwanted young shoots are best rubbed off as soon as they appear. Coral spot disease can be serious on this tree especially on improperly ripened wood which occurs during cold and wet summers. Wood showing orange red pustules should be removed, cutting back to healthy wood, and all prunings burnt.

Seed, which is freely set and which will ripen in a warm summer, is an easy method of propagation. Bought seed or that collected in gardens that experience hot summers should have boiling water poured over it and allowed to remain in the cooled water for 24 hours before being sown. Fully mature seed, gathered at the end of a cool summer or in a warm summer from fully developed pods which have not yet turned brown, can be sown direct without pre-treatment. While seed sown under the protection of a glasshouse or frame will germinate in gentle heat in about two weeks, seed sown directly into the garden in spring may have erratic and delayed germination. Replant seedlings a year later just before they come into growth.

Kingcup

Caltha palustris is widespread throughout the cool, temperate regions of Europe, Asia and North America, in a number of forms or botanical varieties. It occurs in moist ground, in bogs, along the edges of streams, rivers, ponds and lakes, in ditches and water meadows, extending from sea level to alpine meadows. The generic name is derived from a Greek word meaning 'cup' whilst the specific epithet means 'boggy'; these meanings, together with the golden flower colour and time of flowering are responsible for many of the common names. This flower was always associated by country folk with the Virgin Mary, and this is indicated by 'mary' being part of some of the names: 'marygold', 'marybud', 'marsh marigold', 'mayblobs', 'blobs', 'water blobs', 'waterboat', 'water boots', 'boots', 'meadow boots', 'meadowboats', 'gold stud', 'water buttercup', 'golden flower', 'goolds', 'goulds', 'cuckoo buds', 'care', 'drunkards', 'bull flower', 'crazies', 'hobble-gobble', 'bel-boutons', 'publicans-and-sinners', 'bubligans', 'king-of-the-meadows', 'meadow bright', 'meadow bout', and 'wild fire' are just some of the names in English. Two alternative derivations are given for 'kingcup': its resemblance to a golden royal stud, and its status as the king of buttercups. When there are so many different common names for one plant, there is a definite case for a single botanical name, even if it takes a little more effort to pronounce.

Although some flowers can be found at almost any season in the Northern Hemisphere, the best and most impressive display is in April and May; in the past, flowers have been used in May Day celebrations.

Kingcup seems to have been grown in gardens more for its beauty than its usefulness, although it did have some uses: its leaves were used to heal green wounds, and it was said to cure by signature horsebites, because the shape of the leaf resembled a horse-shoe; it was also used as a cure for melancholy. Young leaves were shredded for pottage, while fresh flowers were added to salads and were pickled or candied for use at other seasons. In North America kingcup was called 'cowslip', and cowslip greens were cooked leaves, eaten as a vegetable.

In the garden, kingcup has often occurred naturally where there is water, although it has long been planted in moist soil for its bright golden flowers. The so-called white (really sulphur yellow) has always been highly prized, and it remains as rare today as it ever has been. It is, though, the double flowered form which has found favour from the time it was introduced during the sixteenth century to the present day. While double flowers may not please everyone, the pretty arrangement of the petals in the double kingcup will appeal even to the bigot. In 1597 Gerard wrote that it was a plant new to England which had recently arrived from Germany, while Camerarius, writing at about the same time in Germany, was saying

82

that it had recently come out of England.

Even though the kingcup grows naturally in a wet soil, the double form will grow satisfactorily in any garden soil that is cool and does not dry out during the summer. It may be planted in groups amongst shrubs, at the front of a herbaceous border or island bed or in a shady pocket of a rock garden. Prepare the ground for late spring planting by incorporating as much well rotted organic matter, leaf mould or peat as possible. During the first summer, especially if the soil is dry apply water until the plants have established. Kingcups are increased by division after the main spring flush is over.

Laburnum

Today, 'Laburnum' is the generic name for two trees: *Laburnum anagyroides* and *L. alpinum*, although Linnaeus had in 1753, called them *Cytisus laburnum* and *C. alpinus*. 'Laburnum' has come to be the most frequently used common name but others that are, or have been used are: 'golden rain', 'golden drop', 'gold chain', 'bean trefoil', 'beancod' and 'peascod'.

Laburnum anagyroides (L. vulgare) takes its specific epithet from an allied genus of leguminous plants, *Anagaris*, which was an old generic name for laburnum, used in the sixteenth and seventeenth centuries. This species of *Laburnum* is widespread in southern and central Europe, while *L. alpinum* has a more limited distribution in the Alps, the Apennines and Yugoslavia. Both were probably introduced into Britain originally by the Romans, but they were to be repeatedly reintroduced over the centuries by travellers who were attracted by the tree's beauty at flowering time, and who were to carry back seed. So widespread in England is *L. anagyroides* that it has the adjective 'common' attached to it, and is considered by many to be a British native tree. *L. alpinum* favours a wetter soil and cooler conditions and is more widely grown in northern England and in Scotland, where it has become so common that it has taken unto itself the name 'Scottish laburnum'. The laburnums were being grown in England during the sixteenth century, and while some seventeenth century writers record them, not all do. Perhaps this was because there were so few uses for a tree that had poisonous seeds; the only virtue that seems to be recorded is the use of their leaves in a poultice to reduce swellings. In the Middle Ages, laburnum trees were coppiced to produce strong and durable stems which were used for fencing and screens, and also for making into bows. Seasoned timber is hard, and heartwood is dark in colour; it has been used for making spindles, pulleys, blocks and cogs, as well as furniture. Trees played little part in the layout of sixteenth and seventeenth century gardens, which were composed of a series of small enclosed areas of formal design.

Laburnum would be too large to fit into these, and too small to be used for planting avenues, but they were pleached to make screens, pallisades, arbours, bowers and archways. There was a more extensive planting of laburnums during the eighteenth century because they fitted into a naturalistic landscape, which replaced the formality of the previous two centuries. Following the Industrial Revolution, when towns and cities expanded, laburnum came to be widely planted because its small size was more suited to restricted space and it was well able to tolerate atmospheric pollution.

In almost 300 years a number of selections have been made: weeping forms, leaves totally or margined with yellow, or with leaflets puckered or deeply cut; trees which produced a second flowering in autumn, double flowers and fragrant flowers. It is unlikely that many of these could be found in a nursery today. A hybrid between the two species *L. X watereri* originated at the Knaphill nursery of John Waterer, but it was from a selection of this same cross, made in Holland and known as *L. vossii*, which is the finer and better known, for its flower chains can reach 24in. (600mm).

A novelty whose common name of 'pink laburnum' has attracted many buyers has invariably proved on flowering to be a disappointment, for its flowers, although different in colour, are not as large or impressive as the common or Scottish laburnum. This tree is erroneously referred to as a graft hybrid and although it arose as an accident following grafting, there has in fact been no sexual union of gametes. +*Laburnocytisus adamii*, more correctly a graft chimaera, commemorates Jean Louis Adam in whose Paris nursery it arose in 1825. At that period it was common practice to raise standards of purple broom (*Cytisum purpurea*) by grafting onto the top of 6ft (2m) stems of common laburnum. On one occasion, after the graft had taken, an accident occurred and the scion was broken off above the union. From the remaining embedded portion, a bud developed and the flowers on the resulting branch proved to be pink; tissue of the laburnum had surrounded that of the purple broom so that at flowering the inner purple tissue was seen through a skin of yellow, so producing pink. An analogy might be a lady wearing a pair of thin yellow silk gloves through which her pink skin can be seen. A tree of +*L. adamii* when not in flower resembles that of the common laburnum in appearance, but at flowering as well as branches with pink flowers, there may also be some with yellow and tufts of purple broom flowers. It is necessary to remove the branches with yellow flowers; as they grow at a faster rate than the pink they may come to dominate the tree. It is not necessary to go back to the cumbersome and elaborate procedure which resulted in the original cross to propagate this plant; cuttings taken from branches with pink flowers will produce saplings with pink flowers.

Laburnums make small trees up to 20ft (6m) and so are suited to small or medium sized gardens. They are easy trees to grow and will tolerate most soils which are not waterlogged. Whilst the Scottish laburnum prefers an acid soil which does not dry out, the common laburnum will grow equally well in an acid or an alkaline soil, including one which is shallow and dry. Following winter planting, stake the young tree so that it can be trained into a straight, young trunk. Young and semi-mature trees are prone to attack by rabbits and hares who chew away the bark at or near ground level; protect against these pests with wire netting. Flowering, which takes place in mid-spring, can be profuse, and there are few more beautiful sights than a tree draped with chains of golden flowers. Following good flowering, there can be an excessive seed set which if left to develop can reduce the vigour of the tree. The seed, poisonous to humans and animals, should be removed before it has a chance to develop. As the tree flowers on the previous season's growth, pruning immediately after flowering will remove the poisonous seeds and direct the tree's energy into strong new growth which will bear next year's flowers. Cut back all shoots which have borne flowers to within four or five buds of the previous year's growth. An alternative time to prune is when the tree is fully dormant during the winter. Regular pruning will reduce the size of the tree, produce better flowering and enhance the quality of the blooms. Avoid cutting into old wood which can result in disease infection, spreading to main limbs and the trunk, and once established is difficult to control.

Propagation is by seed or cuttings. A few pods out of the reach of children can be allowed to develop and if gathered as the seed pods turn brown but before they split naturally, will, sown in gentle heat germinate in two or three weeks. Old seed should have boiling water poured over it and be allowed to stand in the cooled water for 24 hours before sowing. For those with a glasshouse, cuttings of young growth taken in late summer are not difficult to root. Cuttings taken in winter of naked young growth can be rooted in the open garden. Select the shoots from the prunings and cut into lengths of about 10in. (250mm); make a slit trench 6–8in. (150–200mm) deep and push the cuttings into it so that only a quarter to a third protrudes, then tread the soil firmly against the cuttings. Rooting should have taken place by the following spring when the buds begin to shoot and grow away.

Lady's Smock

Cardamine pratensis, a common European plant of stream and river banks, is found in wet meadows throughout Britain. It was recorded as being found in abundance on Hampstead Heath in 1629 by Thomas Johnson; one wonders if it is still there today? This perennial plant is related to the watercress, having similar pinnate leaves, but with stems of flowers which are occasionally pure white but are more usually tinged with the faintest pink, and there are also flowers that are purple or deep mauve. Gerard and Parkinson grew this plant in their gardens, both preferring its double form. Parkinson remarks that the double was found frequently in places all over England, and cites Mitcham, only eight miles from London, as an example. In Lancashire it was 'found by the industrie of a worthy gentlewoman dwelling in those parts theretofore remembered, called Mistress Thomasin Tunstall, a great lover of these delights'. As with all plants at this period, both single and double forms also had to have other uses than garden decoration. In the kitchen, the leaves were used as an alternative to watercress in salads or chopped and put into pottage just before serving. Flowers too were added to salads; fresh in springtime or dried or candied at other seasons. All herbalists recommended it as a cure for, or a protection against, scurvy. A lotion made from the plant was used to remove blemishes, spots, pimples and freckles, while mixed with oil it was beneficial for coughs, shortness of breath and pains in the chest. Chewing of the fresh leaves was a cure for toothache and Dioscorides had recommended the juice extracted from them to mollify sunburn.

The 'lady' in 'lady's smock' may be a shortened form of Our Lady, referring the the Virgin Mary to whom the plant is dedicated; another derivation of 'lady's smock' may be that article of clothing worn by shepherdesses, which was the same colour as the flowers; or it may come from the fact that these flowers can be so common in some water meadows that from afar they look like laundered clothes put there to dry. Other common names include: 'milk' or 'milky' 'maids' or 'maidens', 'wild' or 'meadow cress', 'May flower', 'cuckoo flower', 'pink', 'spink', 'boo pink', 'pleasant-in-sight' and 'bread-and-butter'; and this is yet another plant which has been called 'Canterbury bells'. It is mentioned several times in Shakespeare's plays, although the best remembered must be from Love's Labours Lost:

When daisies pied and violets blue
And cuckoobuds of yellow hue
And Lady's smock all silver white
Do paint the meadows with delight.

The colour of the double flower is not mentioned by seventeenth century writers, but it is assumed that it must have been white. In Miller's *Gardeners Dictionary* of 1768, and Mawe and Abercrombie's *The Universal Gardener and Botanist* of 1797, both white and purple doubles are recorded. In *Flora Historica* of 1826, Henry Phillips recommended the single for banks of brooks and lakes, and for the wilderness, while he says that the double may be planted in the front of shrubberies especially amongst evergreens. Reginald Farrer gave it his seal of approval in his

English Rock Garden of 1919 'Lady's Smock remains one of the best, and its double form is a really desirable plant for a cool border amazingly profuse and effective in flower and no less generous with self-sown seedlings which come true to their parent'. This is a surprising observation, for all other references in books over almost 400 years say that the double can only be increased by division, best carried out in the autumn.

In today's gardens the single form might be allowed to colonise the banks of a stream or pond, but even then it should be treated with caution, for with its profuse seeding, it is invasive as well as beautiful and the ground may be needed for more desirable plants. If the double (white with a hint of pink) can be found in a nursery, it is well worth growing for it does not seed itself in spite of what Farrer has to say. While it will grow best in similar conditions to those recommended for the single, it is quite happy when planted in a cool moist soil, and is well suited for planting in groups in a shrubbery, to bloom in the spring, as recommended by Henry Phillips.

Lily-of-the-Valley

Lily-of-the-valley, a rare native of Britain today, was once common. In 1597, Gerard wrote of it being common on Hampstead Heath; it was still there in 1658, according to William Coles, but Philip Miller in 1738 was saying that it was no longer to be found.

In *Convallaria majalis,* the generic name is derived from the Latin and means 'a valley', whilst the specific epithet indicates May flowering. Either or both of these meanings are to be found in some of the alternative English names: 'lily convally', 'lily-in-the valley', 'valley lily', 'May lily', 'May blossom', 'May flower', while there is also: 'lily constancy', 'lily confancy', 'liri cofacy', 'wood lily', 'mugget', 'glovewort', 'white bells', 'fairy bells' and 'dangle-bells'. It was one of the earliest flowers of the English countryside to be taken into gardens, and has retained a place there throughout successive centuries while fashions have come and gone. In its early days it was much used in medicine: Gerard records that if a vase of flowers was put into an ant-hill for a month, then the liquor could be used as a cure for gout. William Coles; six ounces of water of the flowers helpeth those that are poisoned or bit with a mad dog, and being drunk fourty daies it doth away with the falling sickness'. Etmuller, a German physician and botanist of Leipzig, wrote: 'Of the dried flowers of the lily-of-the-valley and the leaves of marjoram, a drachm each in powder, mix them well together with half a scruple of the essential oil of marjoram and use it as snuff'.

Although, in earlier centuries, plants grown in a garden had to be useful, the lily-of-valley was always considered for its beauty and it was grown by all the best known gardeners of the seventeenth century. As well as flowers of the usual white, there were also pink flowers variously described as: blush, red and scarlet; were these all different or were they the same colour? Today there is grown in gardens a form known as 'Roseum' which, although pink in bud, has open flowers which are a dingy mauve; could this be the same plant? At the beginning of the nineteenth century one form is described as having white flowers variegated with pale purple, and in addition to singles white, pink and variegated, there seem also to have been double forms of all these. In 1871 there is mention of a form in which the leaves had golden veins, and sometime later there appeared a form which had a golden margin; both are known today. It was during the nineteenth century that lily-of-the-valley became a commercial florists' flower, and each May large quantities of cut flowers were sold. To extend the season plants were forced, to supply the market with flowers during winter and early spring; these were mostly imported from the Leipzig area of Germany. There had been selection and breeding to produce better forcing kinds with longer stems and larger flowers of a purer white which flowered over a long period. As a florists' flower it remained fashionable until the Second World War, but since 1945 its popularity has faded right away.

In nature this is a woodland plant, and in a garden it grows best in light shade provided by trees and shrubs, although it will grow satisfactorily in full sun. Tolerant of a wide range of soil types as long as neither too wet nor too dry, it does benefit from an adequate supply of organic matter. There are underground rhizomes which spread rapidly and quickly to colonise fresh ground while the older the central portions decline in vigour and freedom of flowering. The underground rhizomes have great powers of penetration, for their shoots can push up through bitumen paths. During the winter these underground rhizomes are dormant, but in spring they push up shoots composed of two lance-shaped leaves vertically rolled with a triangular flower stem emerging at their side. The deliciously fragrant flowers are followed by small spherical orange or scarlet berries to produce an autumn display, but beware for these are poisonous. Seed extracted from these fruits and washed in cold water can be used to raise new plants, but these have a complicated germination process and it can be a very long time before seedlings appear.

As a ground cover amongst shrubs or in a woodland garden, lily-of-the-valley can be left to its own devices, but elsewhere in a garden it needs confining to prevent encroachment. When being grown just for cut flowers, clumps should be lifted every three or four years and pulled apart selecting the strongest shoots from the outside of the clumps to be replanted in well enriched soil, with the rhizomes just covered.

Maize

Maize came into England sometime during the sixteenth century, being first described in Henry Lyte's 1578 translation from the French of *A Nievve Herbal,* originally written in Dutch and German by Rembert Dodoens in 1554. Almost all European writers of herbals of the sixteenth and seventeenth centuries describe maize, often illustrated by woodcuts. None of them, however, was certain of its origin: for India, Turkey, Asia in general, West Indies, South and North America were all suggested, the New World being the favourite. Even today the country of origin may only be speculative for its use as a food crop was widespread in the New World, among the Incas of Peru, the Indians of Nicaragua, the Aztecs of Mexico and the North American Indians. It seems most likely that *Zea mays* came from Mexico, although it is more than probable that it was of hybrid origin.

The first Europeans to see maize were the Spaniards who had accompanied Colombus, and it was on one of his trips of exploration that seed was collected and taken back to Spain, where it was recorded as being in cultivation near Madrid as early as 1525. An interesting suggestion has been made that the Spanish were not the first Europeans to see maize, but that it had been seen centuries earlier by the Vikings; they are now considered to have been the first Europeans to visit America, and they seem to have penetrated as far south as what is now Virginia. The kind of maize illustrated by some of the early woodcuts is a type very similar to one being cultivated by the Indians of eastern North America. Maize had followed European settlement throughout the warmer parts of North America, where it was to become a staple crop. It is now widespread in all the warmer countries of the world as an important cereal.

From what can be read in the herbals of the sixteenth and seventeenth centuries, it seems obvious that it did not find much favour as a food crop. In 1597, John Gerard wrote,

'Turky wheat doth nourish far lesse than either wheat, rie, barley or otes. The bread made thereof is meanly white without bran; it is hard and dry as Bisket and hath in it no clamminesse at all for which cause it is hard of digestion and yieldeth to the body little or no nourishment, it slowly decendeth and bindeth the belly . . . the barbarous indians which know no better, are constrained to make a virtue of necessitie and think it a good food whereas we may easily judge that it nourisheth but little and is hard and evil of digestion, a more convenient food for swine than for men'.

In the next 250 years there are only a few mentions made in gardening books of maize being in cultivation. Philip Miller, in his *Dictionary of Gardening* published in 1738 dismisses maize in similar vein to Gerard: 'The plants are seldom cultivated in England for use but in Italy and Germany it is the food of poor inhabitants . . . At all times will be found a hearty food for cattle, hogs and poultry'. One wonders when maize came to be used to produce that American sweetmeat, popcorn, which has never achieved the same popularity in Europe that it has in the United States.

In the United States in 1779, a new kind of maize appeared in which cobs were harvested while still immature and the unripe but succulent seeds were eaten lightly cooked as a vegetable. Sweetcorn was slow to gain popularity, but by the last quarter of the nineteenth century, large quantities were being canned, although mainly for home consumption. In the early years of the present century, sweetcorn made its appearance in England, firstly in a can but as it gained in popularity, some cultivation of it as a crop began. In the uncertain English climate, it made little progress until plant breeding produced earlier cropping dwarf kinds which had hybrid vigour. While small quantities are still imported from the warmer countries of Europe, Britain is almost self-supporting in sweetcorn. Since the Second World War it has continued to gain popularity but it has never challenged any of our more traditional vegetables.

So far maize has been written about as a cereal or a vegetable, but for at least a century it has been grown in gardens as an ornamental plant. During the nineteenth century when the new garden fashion of bedding was developing, maize was occasionally included with tender annuals for use as dot plants to give height, or was one of the plants used in tropical bedding. During this period, a number of ornamental forms came to be listed by seedsmen in catalogues: 'Japonica' is a strong growing cv which has white striped variegation; 'Gracillima', also with white variegation, makes a smaller plant and has narrower leaves while in 'Quadricolor', the white variegation is overlaid with pink and purple.

In the years which followed the Second World War, flower arranging became immensely popular. Its disciples began to use a much wider range of plant material for their art than had once been used. Amongst this material was non-flowering shoots of maize, green or variegated, as well as the stems of male flowers. It was however, amongst dry arrangements used for winter decoration that maize came to be mostly used. Arrangements of dried flowers, foliage, fruits and seed capsules may not be to everyone's taste, but at least they are to be preferred to the ubiquitous plastic flowers. In the dried arrangements it was the dried cobs of seed that were used. Whereas in sweetcorn, cobs are eaten whilst immature, for flower arranging these cobs have to develop fully so that the seed is fully ripe and hard. Today in catalogues there are cvs offered in which there is a wide variation is seed colour: cream, yellow, orange, red, brown, blue, purple and almost black, and there are kinds in which cobs have multicoloured grains. There is a curious form known as strawberry corn, with small cobs shaped like the fruit, and grains of darkish red. An inference might be made that these are new strains bred within recent years by seedhouses – yet all the colours mentioned here were known to the herbalists of the sixteenth and seventeenth centuries.

——— Marvel of Peru ———

Mirabilis jalapa was brought into Europe by the Spanish conquerors of South America. Gerard had already been growing this plant for many years when he came to write his *Herbal* in 1597. He begins his description of it with: 'This admirable plant called Marvel of Peru or marvell of all the world . . .' Mirabilis is a shortened form of Admirabilis and both spellings of the generic name appear in early garden books. The specific epithet was formerly *peruviana,* an indication of the country of origin, although Peru in the sixteenth and seventeenth centuries was not as precise geographically as it is today. When Linnaeus came to classify the plant in 1753 he chose *jalapa* as the specific epithet because he thought it to be the plant from which jalap, a drug, was obtained; in this he was mistaken, for that plant was in fact *Convolvulus jalapa.* Linnaeus was only one of a number of renowned botanists who had made this same, mistake; Clusius, Boerhave, Tournefort, Lumière and Cornutus all fell for it.

This plant, from sub-tropical South America, is a perennial, with an underground rootstock. It can be treated as such in the colder parts of Europe, where these tubers are lifted and stored over the winter like those of the dahlia, but because it will flower in the first year when raised from seed, it is normally treated as an annual. It produces rather fleshy jointed stems with opposite pairs of lance-shaped leaves. There are terminal heads of flowers, each of which unfolds in late afternoon, remains open throughout the night but is closed and withered next morning, to be followed later the same day by other flowers. This opening of flowers late in the day has been responsible for some of its common names: 'four-o-clock plant/flower', 'belle-de-nuit' translated as 'beauty of the night'. It is one of the number of plants with a nocturnal habit that have been referred to as 'commutor' plants. When it was realised that it was not the source of true jalap, another common name became 'false jalap'.

Gerard mentioned two flower colours, white and yellow; 150 years later Philip Miller added purple ranging to white, and red to yellow. What so excited sixteenth and seventeenth century gardeners was the large number of flower colours, self or striped, dotted or variegated. There could be different flower colours on the same plant, and even in one flower the petals may not all be of the same colour. It has been noticed that seed collected from plants having flowers of one colour could produce seedlings with different coloured flowers. Perhaps this change of flower colour is caused by the low temperatures which are experienced in colder Europe, for in warm countries flower colour seems much more constant. In many warm temperate or sub-tropical countries this plant can be seen along roadsides as a weed on waste or cultivated ground.

During the nineteenth century, marvel of Peru was one of the plants that came to be included in the new fashion of summer bedding because of its long flowering period, which can continue from early summer until frosts arrive. It did not retain its popularity, though, perhaps because it was difficult to obtain plants with just one flower colour. Besides being grown outside in annual borders or in groups for island beds and herbaceous borders, it has been grown in pots to decorate cold conservatories. Henry Phillips in *Flora Historica* recommended it for the decoration of houses when evening entertainments were to take place:

The plants when forced and cultivated in large pots, are well calculated to decorate the saloons of the gay, for however timid the flowers may appear in meeting the smiles of God of Day, they stand the blaze of the strongest artificial light as cheerfully as other belles who delight to shine at the same hour with the emblem of timidity.

In the language of flowers, marvel of Peru is the symbol of timidity.

Although it has continued to be grown in gardens during the twentieth century, it has never been in great favour but has been retained in cottage gardens perhaps as a curiosity. It has increased in importance in recent years as a plant for suburbia, so that people working in towns and cities have something to welcome them on their return home. Seed can be sown in gentle heat in early spring with the seedlings being handled as soon as they are large enough, preferably one to a small pot. Keep under protection until late spring when the danger of frost has passed. Earlier flowering will result from roots lifted at the end of the previous autumn and overwintered in a frost-free shed; these are best potted in spring so that they have begun to grow before they are put out.

Mezereon

Daphne mezereum is a small, deciduous shrub which extends through Europe into Asia, but can occur locally elsewhere in cool temperate countries as a garden escape. Although considered by some botanists as native to the British Isles, and is on this country's protected plant list, it seems almost certain that in the few localities in which plants are recorded, they have come there as escapes from cultivations.

Daphne, a nymph pursued by the lecherous Apollo, was changed into a plant for her own protection. Originally it had been intended to use *Daphne* for the true laurel (now *Laurus nobilis*), but as a generic name it came to be transferred to the present group because of the laurel's similarity to *D. laureola*, the spurge laurel, and to other evergreen species. *Mezereum* is derived from a Persian word meaning 'destroyer of life', a reference to the poisonous nature of all parts of the plants. 'Mezereon' now seems to be the only common name for this plant, although in earlier centuries it might have been prefixed by 'Dutch', for it was from Holland that most of the plants sold in English nurseries came; two other old names are 'German spurge' and 'dwarf bay'.

Surprisingly, there is no mention of mezereon by William Turner, Nicholas Culpepper or William Coles. John Gerard recommends it as a drastic cure for the alcoholic: 'if a drunkard do eat one graine or berry of the plant, he cannot be allured to drinke one drinke at that time such is the heat of the mouth and choking in the throat'; he goes on to warn of its poisonous properties. At that time, though, roots were chewed to alleviate toothache and an infusion of the roots was used by ladies when dieting.

Even though it is a plant for which the herbalists found few virtues, it has always been much planted in gardens. In Britain and the colder parts of Europe, any plant which flowers in winter will be appreciated and one that is also brightly coloured with fragrant flowers will become much esteemed. Gerard, Parkinson, Rea, Evelyn and Sir Thomas Hanmer all mention this plant and record flowers that were white, common blush, peach and red; in the eighteenth century John Abercrombie adds crimson and purple, and one form that had variegated foliage. With its fragrant and colourful flowers produced in winter, it has retained its place in British gardens, although more often in cottage gardens than in those of the wealthy. In recent years it has fallen out of fashion because of infection by a mosaic virus which causes flecking and blotching of the leaves, loss of vigour and sudden death.

Mezereon has a place in a winter garden, the front of a shrub border or on a large rock garden. Because it does not transplant well when bare rooted, it is usually sold in small containers, but when buying do ensure that these are not starved or rootbound. Although planting can take place throughout most of the year, early spring is best, and small plants, if not rootbound, will quickly establish and grow away. A little light pruning following planting and in early years will help to establish a sound framework; this consists of removing the apical bud or pinching out the growing point on young shoots. Hard pruning should be avoided on established bushes. The soil in which mezereon is to be grown should be well prepared with the incorporation of organic matter and an annual mulch of well decayed compost in early spring is beneficial.

Propagation is by seed with coloured flower forms coming mostly true. The white flowered form has yellow berries which the birds avoid, although they will strip the red berries produced by all other forms even before these are fully ripe. Extract the seed from the fruits and wash in cold water before sowing immediately outside or in pots plunged in the open garden, with germination occurring as temperatures rise in the spring. Pot the seedlings as soon as they are big enough to handle, one to a small pot using a mixture of equal parts of soil, sand and peat; plant into a permanent position in the following spring, however small the plants.

Michaelmas Daisies

'Michaelmas daisy' has come to be used for several plants belonging to the genus *Aster* which flower in gardens in late summer and autumn. The first of these to be grown in England was *Aster amellus* which was introduced in the sixteenth century. At that time it had the botanical name of *Aster atticus* and the common names of 'Italian starwort' or 'Italian marigold', as an indication of the country from which it came. In England it came to be called 'blue starwort' to separate it from the common starwort (*A.*

tripolium), a native of sea marshes around the British coast which had yellow flowers. This plant tended to languish in gardens until the latter part of the nineteenth century when William Robinson introduced the garden fashion of herbaceous borders. Although it reached a peak of popularity in the years between the wars, it is still widely grown today for cut flowers or in herbaceous borders or island beds. Its stems reach about 2ft (600mm), with a much branched head of flowers up to 3in. (75mm) in diameter in a range of colours: shades of pink, purple and blue, and also white.

Any plant which is called 'Michaelmas daisy' would be expected to be, in flower on the day devoted to the archangel: 29th September in the new calendar, while in the old calendar it was 10th October. Philip Miller called *Aster tradescantii* 'Michaelmas daisy' although in the previous century it had been called 'Virginian aster'. From the specific epithet, it would be assumed that this plant had been introduced into England by John Tradescant, who had made his first trip to the New World in 1637. This plant, though, is recorded by Thomas Johnson in his revision of Gerard's *Herbal* of 1633, in which he says he had got it from John Tradescant, so although it was not introduced by Tradescant it was distributed from his garden at Lambeth. Now less common in gardens, it reaches about 4ft (1.3m) and has large heads of tiny white daisy flowers. It has been largely superseded in twentieth-century gardens by other species with larger and brighter flowers, but it does have the redeeming feature of being one of the last plants in the herbaceous border to flower.

Today 'Michaelmas daisy' is retained as the name for *A. novi-belgii* and its hybrids, which flower in late summer and early autumn, although they have long finished blooming by Michaelmas. This plant, which can reach 4ft (1.3m) has also produced a race of dwarfs less than 2ft (600mm) and has flowers in a range of shades of pink, mauve and purplish blue as well as white, with doubles as well as singles. The name is also used for *A. novae-angliae* which does not come into flower until a month after the previous species and which it overtops by a foot (300mm); this species seems to have only mauve and pink flowers. The specific epithet in *A. novi-belgii* refers to New Holland, an early name for New York State, and 'New York aster' has been a common name for this plant, while 'New England aster' has also been a common name for the other species. Both *A. novi-belgii* and *A. novae-angliae* are said to have been introduced into England in 1710, yet a plant under this latter name was being grown by Doctor Robert Morison in the physic garden at Westminster in about 1650; it may be that in *A. novae-angliae*, it was not intended that novae-angliae be a specific epithet but an indication of the plant's origin. In 1633 Thomas Johnson, in his revision of Gerard's *Herbal* included as a footnote *Aster virginicus fruticosus minor,* which might be *A. novi-belgii*.

Irrespective of when these two species arrived in Britain, it was not until the closing years of the nineteenth century that they made any impact in gardens. William Robinson took up the cause of this genus which he felt had been too long neglected, and organised a conference to discuss them in 1891. It was, though, Ernest Ballard, a nurseryman with a nursery at Colwell who developed *A. novi-belgii,* so that it was to become one of the most important flowers in a garden for late summer display. It is curious that this species should have produced such a large number of cvs of differing heights and size of flowers in a wide colour range, whereas there has been scarcely any improvement in *A. novae-angliae*. Michaelmas daisies have largely fallen from fashion in recent years due to the devastation of tarsonemid mite and mildew on forms of *A. novi-belgii* although other species seem to be unaffected.

Michaelmas daisies are easy to cultivate and seem indifferent to soil. Plant in groups in a herbaceous border or island bed, position and space according to height and kind. The best flowering comes from young healthy clumps, with performance falling off if these are left undisturbed for too many years. Lift every third year during the winter, chop the clumps into pieces, discarding the central portions and replant into well prepared ground.

Mignonette

It is curious that mignonette seems so completely out of favour in gardens today, when flower fragrance is considered to be an essential characteristic. In his *Flora Historica* of 1824, Henry Phillips wrote:

It is not yet an age since this fragrant weed in Egypt first perfumed the European gardens yet it has so far naturalised itself to our climate as to spring from seed on its own scattering and thus convey its delightful odour from the parterre of the prince to the most humble garden of the cottager. In less than another age we predict (without the aid of Egyptian art) that the children of our peasants will gather these luxurious little plants amongst the wild flowers of our hedgerows.

It would be interesting to know how many years Henry Phillips considered to be an age! *Reseda odorata* had first come to Europe and into France in the early years of the eighteenth century, where it was to become known as mignonette which means 'little darling'. Even the English, who abhor foreign words, have retained the French common name and in fact have transferred it to a native British plant, *R. luteola,* which for centuries had been called 'dyer's weed': now this is more usually referred to as 'wild mignonette'. The popularity of mignonette in France is said to date from the time of Napoleon's conquest of Egypt when he had seed sent back to

Single China Aster

Mignonette

Josephine so that she could raise plant for her garden at Malmaison. It became widely grown in southern France where its flowers were used for making perfume. Many books of reference give the date of introduction into England as 1752, when Philip Miller was growing it in the Chelsea Physic Gardens in London. There is, however, a footnote on a manuscript written by Sir Joseph Banks that plants in England had arisen from seed obtained by Lord Bateman from the Royal Gardens in Paris and sent to his kinsman Mr Richard Bateman at Old Windsor in 1742. In England it soon became popular, especially in the capital where it seemed well able to cope with the atmospheric pollution of London. So common did it become in window boxes that Henry Phillips said 'We have frequently found the perfume of mignonette so powerful in some of the better streets of London that we have considered it sufficient to protect the inhabitants from those effluvia which bring disorders in the air'. At this time it was being grown for cold conservatory decoration and Henry Phillips was also re-commending it as a pot plant for decorating homes when evening entertainments were to take place. Its use as a pot plant was to continue into the twentieth century and even in the years after the Second World War, large quantities were being sold in Covent Garden. During the nineteenth century breeding had been taking place in England and the USA to produce improved forms especially suitable for pot culture as well as for garden use. More upright and branched forms with longer spikes of flowers were produced, the greenish or whitish yellow flowers were increased in size, and cvs were produced which had flowers of a brighter yellow as well as red; the machet strain became especially used for pot work.

Reseda odorata is a perennial plant (although usually treated as an annual) which occurs in many countries of North Africa, extending into Turkey. In many of the warmer countries, it has escaped from gardens so that the species seems to have a much wider distribution. The generic name is derived from the Latin and means 'to heal'.

Although Pliny refers to a plant as *Reseda* which was used for its curative properties, there is no mention of any of the few European species being used by herbalists of the sixteenth and seventeenth centuries. Mention has already been made of one English species, *R. luteola*, from which a dye was obtained.

It is interesting to speculate why this plant which was so very common in gardens up to 30 years ago has fallen so completely out of favour. Certainly it has an untidy habit, its flowers are small, short lived and rather dull but its strong perfume ought to have outweighed these disadvantages. Now that there has been a revaluation of flower colour and the brightest and most garish are no longer considered as the most desirable perhaps this deliciously scented plant will return to favour.

Although seedlings can be raised under glass for planting into the garden in late spring, in warmer gardens it is preferable to sow the seed direct where they are to flower. When the seedlings are large enough to handle, they can be thinned to stand 6–10in. (150–250mm) apart.

Musk Hyacinth

In the seventeenth century, hyacinth was a more general name that it is today and included, besides the hyacinth we know, species of *Scilla* referred to as 'starry hyacinths' (sometimes written as iacinth or jacinth) and what we now call *Muscari* which included grape hyacinths & fair-haired hyacinths. Gerard in his *Herbal* wrote of two plants which he referred to as *Muscari flava* or 'yellow musked grape-flower' and *M. clussi,* which was called 'ash coloured grape flower'. In *Paradisus in Sole; Flora, Pomona and Ceres* and *Museum Tradescantium,* Parkinson, Rea and Tradescant have also *Muscari flore-albo* or 'white musk grape flower'. Linnaeus in *Species Plantarum* of (1753) was to use *Hyacinthus muscari,* a name that was to remain in use until 1813 when it was reclassified in the genus *Muscari.*

In later centuries the yellowish flowered form came to be referred to as 'musk hyacinth' under the name of *Muscari moschatum* where genus, specific epithet and common name all refer to the strong fragrance of the flower. The genus *Muscari* has suffered much at the hands of that part of the botanical fraternity known as splitters; in recent years there have been very many name changes but the wheel has turned full circle and most species are once again back in *Muscari. M. moschata* now becomes *M. muscarimi* (the specific epithet in this name is derived from the Turkish for the musk-like fragrance) but it is described as 'white flowered' and so would be the plant that the seventeenth century writers referred to as *M. flore-albo,* while the yellow form in now known as *N. macrocarpum* and Gererd's ash coloured grape flower or *M. clusii* is most probably *M. ambrosiacum.*

What we have long known as *M. moschatum,* a name still retained in many bulb catalogues, was the first species to come into European gardens from Turkey in the second half of the sixteenth century. Flowers had been seen by the European diplomatic corps in the gardens of the Ottoman court of Suleiman the Magnificent. Bulbs of the musk hyacinth along with tulips and Asian ranunculus had been sent home by Ogier Ghislain de Busbecq to his master Ferdinand of Austria whence it became distributed throughout Europe, and it was well established in English gardens before the end of the century. Although widely grown in seventeenth-century gardens, it declined in popularity in the eighteenth and even in the nineteenth century it seems to have been little considered. A number of comments which appear in books of the period are similar to that expressed by William Robinson in 1870:

This is so deliciously sweet-scented and withal so decidedly ugly that it ought long ago to have been a favourite with authors of books on the Language of Flowers, so suggestive is it of merit under the plainest exteriors. When it comes in flower in March and April according to warmth of season or position, the flowers, larger than those of the blue kind, are of such an indescribably unattractive tone of livid greenish yellow . . .'

Even if the musk hyacinth did not find favour in high places, it was more common in cottage gardens. When fragrant flowers are so much in demand in a garden and there is the novelty of colour, it is surprising that musk hyacinth is so uncommon today. A number of species of *Muscari* increase so rapidly that they can become serious weeds; can it be that musk hyacinth has come to be lumped together with those troublemakers which no one wants to grow? In gardens today this expensive bulb increases too slowly, and it takes many years for a single bulb to increase sufficiently to produce a substantial clump. Whilst it grows taller than most other species, it is still small enough to be grown on a rock garden or it can be grown in a container for home or alpine house decoration: It can be planted in a bulb garden or amongst shrubs.

When bulbs are available in the early autumn plant in groups, not singly; select a rather rich well drained soil that is in full sun and plant with the bulbs 1–2in. (25–50mm) below the soil surface. Once planted, bulbs should be left undisturbed and allowed to increase naturally so that big clumps are formed; lift and separate only when they become overcrowded or go into decline in late summer when dormant. There are now also two improved forms, with larger and deeper, purer yellow flowers: *M m. major* and *M. m. flora.*

Myrtle

Myrtle, together with an adjective, has been applied to many woody members of the family Myrtaceae and to identify the original myrtle it has been prefixed by 'common'. *Myrtus communis* was much prized by all the ancient civilisations and is now so widespread in countries around the Mediterranean and beyond that its country (or countries) or origin is uncertain, but is probably one or several in western Asia. Although introduced into Britain by the Romans it did not establish itself in these old islands. Reintroduction probably occurred in the fifteenth or sixteenth century, for it was known in 1548 to William Turner, the father of English botany who was physician at Syon House. With the establishment of gardening as a leisure pursuit for the gentry in the seventeenth century, myrtle became much grown in gardens but usually in containers which were housed in winter. There was a fine collection of myrtles grown by Sir Henry Capel at the White House at Kew, as recorded in the diary of John Evelyn. (It was in the White House that the dowager Princess Augusta was living when she founded a botanic garden nearby which was to become the Royal Botanic Gardens).

Myrtle was the tree and flower associated with love, and was sacred to the Greek goddess Aphrodite and the Roman goddess Venus; in the Christian religion it has been associated with the Virgin Mary. It featured in wedding ceremonies, and sprigs taken from the bridal bouquet were inserted as cuttings in the garden of the newly weds' home; if these rooted and the plants thrived, so would the marriage. White, the colour of myrtle flowers, is the symbolic colour of weddings, although in some countries it is also associated with death, so myrtle has featured in funeral rites.

In the sixteenth and seventeenth centuries myrtle, like many other garden plants, had a variety of utilitarian uses. Bathing in water in which myrtle leaves had been steeped was said to remove unpleasant body odours and helped to set bone fractures and dislocated joints. A lotion made from the flowers was used to bathe eyes, to restore their sparkle and also to improve the sight in elderly people who were suffering from cataracts. Myrtle was used as a cure for three unexpected and widely differing complaints: earache, ulcers and piles. The juice of the berries was used to cure conditions of the head: sores and scabs of the scalp, dandruff, and falling hair and was used as a hair dye. In the kitchen a sauce was made from the berries as an accompaniment to a pig's head.

Although myrtle has long had a reputation in gardens for being tender, it is reasonably hardy in southern England and will survive all but the coldest winters outside. In the more favoured parts of the country some venerable old trees can be found which must be of considerable antiquity. In countries adjacent to the Mediterranean it can make a tree in excess of 12ft (4m), but in England it more usually makes a shrub less than half this height. Evergreen lance-shaped leaves up to 2in. (50mm) × ¾in. (18mm), dark green in colour, are oppositely arranged; if a leaf is held up to the light, it appears to have countless pin-pricks, which are oil glands, and when the leaf is crushed these emit a pleasant fragrance. Flowers are produced in leaf axils, towards the end of summer; these have white petals, but their most noticeable characteristic is the mass of white stamens. Following the flowers, elongated oval fruits develop in most seasons which are black when ripe and long lasting. Over the centuries a number of forms have appeared with leaves of differing lengths and widths, some of which have been variegated with silver or gold: so too have flowers with more than the usual five petals and with varying degrees of doubleness, and fruits which range from white through many shades of red. A naturally occurring form is the tarentum myrtle, *M. communis var tarentina* which makes a small compact shrub, has whitish berries and seems hardier than the type.

Myrtle seems indifferent to soil, but does best in one which is not too rich, is well drained, does not lie wet in winter and contains some lime. It is for a mild garden but in colder areas it will grow satisfactorily if planted and trained against a south facing wall. As has been mentioned it has long been grown in containers which are given protection during the winter, to be stood outside during warmer weather in front of the houses, cafés, on terraces or within the garden because of the fragrant foliage and flowers. These may be shrubs which are trimmed into pillars cones or pyramids or trained to a single stem so as to make a standard to 6ft (2m). Some light pruning is desirable in spring just before new growth begins, when dead and damaged wood is removed, crowded or weak shoots are thinned and the plant is trimmed to shape. Once established, container grown plants should be fed at regular intervals throughout the summer and at no time should watering be neglected. When transferred to protection at the onset of winter, bushes should be kept in a frost-free building where there is plenty of light, and enough water given to keep the soil just moist.

Propagation is by cuttings taken in late summer of non-flowering shoots; when rooted these are kept in frost-free conditions after potting throughout the winter. When the containers have filled with roots, transfer to a larger size and keep the plants growing throughout the summer in a glasshouse. Planting from the container can take place in the following spring or early summer after the danger of spring frost is over.

Nasturtium

Nasturtium is a genus belonging to the family *Cruciferae,* of which watercress (*N. officinale*) is the best known species. As a common name it is applied to two plants from a different family: *Tropaeolum minus* and *T. majus.* Today the latter is much used in a flower garden amongst collections of annuals, as a bedding plant, a temporary filler, in window boxes or for hanging baskets; besides having flowers in a range of bright colours it gives of its best in a poor soil. Today it is grown for ornamentation and yet all parts of the plant can be used as food. The leaves are used in salads, chopped stems or roots added to soups or stews, fresh flowers are put into salads during the summer, or these can be pickled or crystallised for winter use, immature seeds are used as a caper substitute, or the ground, fully ripe seed, when mixed with vinegar, provides a condiment like mustard.

The two plants have a long history in English gardens and have been known under a number of names. Before Linnaeus based his binomial system of classification on floral characteristics, earlier botanists had used other criteria. One was based on practical use and because the taste of the leaves of these species of *Tropaeolum* resembled the watercress, it became *Nasturtium indicum* or Indian cress. 'Indian' here is indicative of the West Indies, which in the sixteenth and seventeenth centuries were less precise geographically than they are today, including besides the Caribbean Islands, parts of Central America and Peru, the country from which the plants originate. Many writers of the seventeenth century used *Nasturtium indicum* or Indian cress, although the two were distinguished by prefixing with 'greater' or 'lesser', sometimes 'major' or 'minor'. Parkinson, however, used 'yellow larks spurr' although some of his contemporaries called them 'yellow larksheele'. Larkspur today is the common name for a summer annual, *Delphinium consolida (Consolida ambigua)* which in the seventeenth century was more often called 'larksheel'. The same common name for plants from quite different families came about from the spurs to be found on the flowers of each. In 1693 John Evelyn had published a book *Compleat Gardner* which was a translation of a French book by La Quintinie, gardener to the French king; he used the name *nasturce* or 'Capucin capers'. Another translation from the French, the *Solitary or Retired Gardener* of 1706, had used monkshood which, like the Evelyn name, seems to suggest the cowls worn by monks. Linnaeus, in *Species Plantarum* of 1753, called the genus *Tropaeolum,* which had been derived from a Greek word for a trophy. Perhaps this was intended to refer to a post set up on a battlefield after combat on which shields and helmets of the defeated were hung; the round leaves were compared to the shields and the flowers to the helmets.

Gerard seems to have been the first person in England to have grown a nasturtium, for there is a mention of one in his catalogue of plants in his Holborn garden of 1596 which was illustrated in his *Herbal* published in the following year. This plant was identified by Linnaeus as *T. minus.* William Aiton, in the first edition of *Hortus Kewensis* of 1789, records that *T. majus* was introduced in 1686 by a Dr Lumley Lloyd. Although every writer afterwards quotes this date of introduction, it must be suspect. In the catalogue of plants grown in the Oxford Botanic Gardens in 1648, Jacob Bobart lists Indian cresses in the plural. In a letter dated 1688, Charles Hatton, in writing to his brother Sir Christopher at Kirby Hall in Northamptonshire, makes reference to seeds of curious plants obtained from Mr Bobart (son of the compiler of the catalogue but also a curator of the Botanic Gardens at Oxford): 'I have sent some seeds of ye large Nasturtium Indicum with a scarlet flower, said to be vivace, because if sown now, it will continue all winter and you may propagate it by slippes. This hath soe disparaged ye other, ye neglect of it will in a few years make it to grow scarce'. It does seem that over a very long period there has been confusion between *T. minus* and *T. majus,* for the descriptions by some authors of one seem to refer to the other.

Gerard gives no virtue for Indian cress, so it can be assumed that it was grown for its attractive flowers, which is borne out by Parkinson: 'a fine small sent very pleasing, which being placed in the middle of some Carnations or Gilliflowers (for they are in flower at the same time) make a delicate Tussimussie, as they call it, or Nosegay, both for sight and sent'. Sir Thomas Hanmer in 1659 and John Rea in 1665 were still growing them in the flower garden, but in 1677, William Lucas in his catalogue includes Indian cress with salads and in 1699 John Evelyn describes it at some length in his book *Acetaria – a discourse of Sallets;* he also mentions its use as a prevention and cure for scurvy. Batty Langley in *New Principles of Gardening* of 1728 was growing the lesser Indian cress on a hot bed, suggesting that there was all-the-year-round production.

While the lesser Indian cress stayed in the kitchen garden during the eighteenth century, the greater seems to have been allowed into the flower garden, and may even have been used for glasshouse decoration. In 1730 Robert Furber in his book *Twelve Months of Flower* illustrated a double yellow, and a set of drawings with the same title by Jacob van Huysum a few years later depicts a double orange. These may have been the two referred to by Phillip Miller in his *Gardener's Dictionary* of 1731 but for which he gives no colours. The range of sterile doubles increased throughout the nineteenth century and were still being grown up to the Second World War, when they were mainly used in bedding; these doubles had to be propagated by cuttings. Although the greater nasturtium seems to have gained in popularity as the range of colours has increased, *T. minus* has remained neglected because it does not seem to have produced any colours other than yellow. There has been hybridisation, of *T. majus* with other species, notably *T. lobbianum,* to extend colours while the non-climbing kinds referred to as 'Tom Thumb' probably resulted from being crossed with *T. minus.* In the twentieth century the small Gleam hybrids have been developed from a plant found in 1930 in a Californian garden which had semi-double yellow fragrant flowers. During the last century there were two cvs at least with coloured foliage: one is described as golden yellow and the other as red. Were these raised from seed or propagated like the doubles from cuttings? In the last ten years a few kinds have been listed by seedsmen which have white flecked leaves; unlike most forms of variegation these come true from seed.

T. majus is offered for sale by seedsmen under a number of cultivar names whilst *T. minus* is difficult to find. The large seeds can be space sown when they are pushed into the ground so that they are about ½in. (12mm) deep. Choose a position in full sun in a poor soil; in shade or a rich soil an excess of leaf growth will hide fewer flowers. Seed can be sown on the sunny side of a hedge which will provide support to the stems which cling with twining leaf stalks; and alternative is to make a wigwam of cut branches to provide support. Often plants are just allowed to sprawl where they can make excellent ground cover. Once established, plants self-sow and seeds falling to the ground naturally germinate more readily when temperatures rise in the spring than do seeds which have been dried.

Paris Daisy

Argyranthemum (Chrysanthemum) frutescens is a Canary Island plant which is a sub shrub and can reach 5ft in height, although in cultivation it is little more than half of this. Much branched, it has alternate deeply lobed, typical chrysanthemum-shaped leaves which vary in shade from green to grey; flowers of the daisy form are little more than an inch (25mm) in diameter and white in colour. It was introduced into European gardens in the sixteenth century and was widely grown in Holland and France for its succession of summer flowers; their long stems made them ideal for cutting, and bunches were sold in quantity in the French capital. It is not surprising, then, that when introduced into England in 1699 it was called 'Paris daisy', although another common name was 'French marguerite'; this, with a number of other plants with daisy-like flowers, commemorates the queen of Henri of Navarre. Because it was not hardy in England, it was grown in pots and tubs which were housed in winter but stood outside on terraces and in parterres during the summer. Towards the end of the eighteenth century and throughout the nineteenth it came to be much used in towns and cities, not only as a plant for pots, tubs and urns but also for window boxes. For more than a hundred years trained plants have been used to grace the entrances to cafés and restaurants in London, for its continuous flowering ensured blooms at all times throughout the summer. With the introduction of the new garden style of bedding early in the nineteenth century, the Paris daisy became an important constituent and its development began. Flower size increased, as did the number of rows of petals and there were full doubles as well as those described as anemone-centred. Whereas the original colour had been white, there were now pinks which ranged from the palest shade to the darkest, and yellows as pale as sulphur or as bright as gold; in these two colours there were anemone-centres and full doubles as well as singles. Unfortunately, most of these have disappeared from English gardens but they are still to be found in the warmer gardens of the Mediterranean countries, North America, New Zealand and the southern states of Australia.

As has been said, this plant needs a garden where winter frosts are light or winter protection in a frost-free glasshouse where just enough water is given to keep it alive. It is not difficult to root if non-flowering shoots are taken, preferably in late summer; as these can be difficult to find at that time, cut hard a few shoots and these will provide plenty of cutting material. Rooted cuttings should be overwintered in a frost-free glasshouse; cuttings taken in springtime will also give good results, although smaller plants at planting out time after the danger of fost is past. Paris daisy is prone to attack by leaf-miner, whose larvae tunnel through leaf tissue producing disfiguring marks and streaks; to deal with this, spray with malathion. It can be used in summer bedding, in groups in herbaceous borders or island beds, for window boxes, tubs troughs or urns. For containers, standard plants may be preferred, on 3ft stems. Pot up separately cuttings which were rooted in spring, providing with each a thin cane to which the main stem is tied; pinch out all side shoots. As one pot fills with roots, transfer to a larger one and as the main stem increases in length replace the thin cane with one that is stronger and taller. Pinch out any side shoots which may develop and remove all flower buds. It is better to keep in a glasshouse until a stem in excess of 3ft has been produced, when side shoots can be allowed to develop; it will take about 18 months to 2 years to reach this size.

Peony

The two species longest in cultivation are the male *(Paeonia mascula)* and the female *(P. officinalis)*, both originating from southern Europe. It has long been thought that the male peony was native to the British Isles for clumps have, at various times, been found in a number of places. In 1597 Gerard reports finding peonies in a field at Gravesend, although Thomas Johnson claimed that Gerard had planted them himself when he revised the *Herbal* in 1633. The Reverend Walter Stonehouse mentions finding a clump in a field in his parish at Darfield in Yorkshire in 1640, but postulates that it had probably come from a garden. Certainly there are clumps on Steepholm, an island in the Bristol Channel, but as there had been a monastery on the island as early as Saxon times, the plants are probably survivors from its garden. Plants are long lived and can be found on the site of an abandoned garden long after the house has disappeared.

Both would have been introduced into Britain by the Romans because of their medicinal properties, for they had been regarded highly by physicians of ancient civilisations around the Mediterranean. The genus commemorates Paeon, a pupil of Asculapius who was the god of medicine amongst the ancient Greeks. Dioscorides and Theophrastus, whose works were to form the basis of medicine in Europe and beyond for more than 1500 years, wrote glowingly about the peony. From herbals of the seventeenth century it can be seen that it effected cures for yellow jaundice, kidney pains, gall stones, epilepsy, falling sickness and internal bleeding; a decoction of the seeds in wine or mead, drunk morning and night, prevented nightmares, counteracted depression and was used for mental illnesses. Ailments of men were cured by the male peony whilst women's illnesses were cured by the female.

As well as for their medicinal uses, peonies have always been esteemed for the beauty of their flowers. The male peony has produced no variation in flower form and colour, it is the female which has always been prized for its beautiful flowers. In the sixteenth century in English gardens, single whites and reds were being grown along with a double red which was more highly valued. Gerard reported hearing of a double white which he was hoping to obtain from Holland and which was to be in many gardens by 1657. Although this double white does not appear in the list of plants that John Tradescant grew at Lambeth, he did have both pink and purple doubles. William Coles, writing in his book *Adam in Eden* in 1657, said that there was a good collection at the Oxford Botanic Gardens (he also mentions one with a yellow flower).

The female peony has retained the affection of gardeners for four centuries, but its development really began at the end of the nineteenth century when herbaceous borders became fashionable. In the early years of the twentieth century it attracted the attention of many nurserymen, who through breeding extended the colour range among both the singles and the various forms of doubles. At present peonies seem to be out of favour, probably because they are difficult to handle by garden centres with modern marketing methods.

Peonies will tolerate a wide range of soils as long as they are not waterlogged. Before planting, soil should be thoroughly prepared with the inclusion of copious quantities of organic matter. Because peonies start into growth early, they are not an ideal choice for cold spring gardens. Plants offered for sale are mostly bare rooted and these should be planted whilst they are dormant in groups at the front of a herbaceous border or island bed. Following planting, it may take a year or two before plants settle down and begin to flower. Some support may be necessary for those with double flowers for the size of the blooms may make them too heavy for their stems. As soon as new growth begins at the end of winter, push in branches of at least three feet in length around the plant; these will provide support to the flower stems without looking unsightly. Once planted, peonies are best left undisturbed as long as they are growing strongly. When lifting the rest of the herbaceous border every third year for division and replanting, dig round the peonies which are left *in situ*.

Propagation can be by division or with pieces taken off the dormant roots. Before growth begins, lift the clump and cut into pieces. Each plump bud with a section of root 4–6in. (100–150mm) can be cut off and inserted into pots or boxes of a sandy compost or lined out in a nursery bed. The singles occasionally produce seed. In any seed capsule there will be a mixture of large plump black seed and small wizened infertile red. Seed can be used to raise new plants but it is unlikely that they will resemble their parents. Seed of peonies can take two or more years to germinate.

Periwinkle

'Periwinkle' is used as a common name for two different plants: lesser periwinkle is *Vinca minor* and the greater is *V. major*. The former is the hardier and can be grown throughout the British Isles while the latter, though completely hardy in the south, is not reliable in the colder parts of the country. Both have long, thin stems which are often woody at the base. In the lesser, there are opposite pairs of narrow oval leaves up to 1½in. (37mm) long and ½–¾in. (12–18mm) wide in a dark green colour, with usually blue flowers up to an inch (25mm) in diameter produced in the leaf axils of new growth. In *V. major,* stems are more vigorous with opposite pairs of leaves which can reach 3in. (75mm) × 2in. (50mm), with larger flowers, usually having narrower petals of a paler blue; seed is very rarely set on cultivated plants of either species.

The old Latin name was *pervinca* which Linnaeus shortened to *Vinca* when he used it for a generic name. Prior to the publication of his *Species Plantarum* in 1753, some botanists had called *V. major 'Clematis daphnoides'*. By the sixteenth century, the Latin *pervinca* became periwinkle, in English variously spelt. Other English names for the lesser periwinkle include: 'blue bell', 'blue Betsy', 'blue button', 'blue bottle', 'blue Jack', 'blue Bill', 'Bill', 'Billy button' and 'cut finger'. Translations from other European languages have produced 'sorcerer's violet', because it was used by witches and warlocks in magic spells; 'flower-of-death' because of its association with funerals and 'flower-of-a-hundred-eyes'. The only alternative name for *V. major* seems to have been 'cockles'.

Both species have a similar distribution in southern and central Europe, Asia Minor and the Caucasus. Although *V. minor* is common throughout Britain and *V. major* is often found apparently growing wild in the south, neither are native plants but have long ago escaped from cultivation, as they have in North America. They were probably brought into England by the Romans, who used them in funeral rites. This association with death seems common in a number of European countries just as it once was in Britain. Periwinkle was planted in graveyards and on graves and the flexuous stems with their evergreen leaves were ideally suited for making into wreathes at any time of the year. Stems of periwinkle were twined around the bodies of young children when laid in their coffins. Garlands of periwinkle were carried in procession to church when a youth or maiden had died and either cast onto the coffin before the grave was filled or hung up in the church. Wreathes of periwinkle were worn by condemned criminals on their way to execution.

A less macabre association is to be found in the language of flowers: periwinkle is the emblem of sincerity and enduring and unalterable friendship. Posies and nosegays were exchanged between friends, and garlands of periwinkle were used to adorn loved ones. Culpepper in his *Herbal* said that leaves eaten together by man and wife caused love between them.

Dioscorides had recommended that an extract of periwinkle drunk in wine would cure internal bleeding and dysentery, while chewing leaves was a cure for toothache. In England in the seventeenth century, periwinkle was used to cure sores and ulcers of the mouth, and a sprig held in the mouth stopped a nosebleed. A poultice of leaves was used to extract the poison from a viper bite. A trail of periwinkle tied round the legs was claimed to cure cramp.

In spite of its uses in medicine throughout the Middle Ages and later, it was at all times appreciated for its pretty flowers. Parkinson wrote: 'The first, blew (the straight species in *V. minor*) groweth in many woods and orchards by the hedgeside in England and so doth the white here and there, but the other single and double purple are in our gardens onely'; there was also mention of a double white. Miller, in the middle of the eighteenth century, was to add two forms with variegated leaves, one with silver and the other gold.

At the present time there is a considerable number of cvs of the lesser periwinkle with a variation in flower colour and form: blue, blue-purple, red-purple and white (sometimes with pinkish shadings to the bud) of varying sizes, single and double in varying degrees. To the usual single blue of the greater periwinkle grown by Gerard and Parkinson, Miller had added one that had white flowers. Today there is far less variation with this species than with *V. minor;* there is in addition to those forms mentioned one of a darker shade of blue, a double blue, and two with variegated leaves:

one has a cream margin and the other has conspicuous gold veins on young leaves which fade or disappear as they age.

As garden plants, periwinkles are used for planting in woodland; in the smaller confines of a cottage garden they are planted in a mixed border. Periwinkles have come into their own during the last 20 years for use as ground cover under trees or shrubs. Both species are tolerant of full sun or deep shade, though flowering is always better when light is good. They are largely indifferent to soil as long as it is not waterlogged.

The lesser periwinkle is probably the more attractive plant and is hardier and therefore the more reliable of the two. It is especially useful for planting on a steep bank which is difficult to manage and can be used as an alternative to grass in glades or for paths in a woodland. When planting for ground cover, put out at 1ft. (300mm) spacing in alternate rows, the same distance apart. Cut back the plants almost to ground level following planting to encourage the production of copious shoots from under the ground. Weeding will be necessary in the early years until a satisfactory cover has been produced, but at any time, perennial weeds which establish themselves should be carefully removed. If a show is to be made of the flowers, a light trim in autumn will allow these to be more easily seen when they are produced in spring; with variegated foliage types, trimming should be carried out in spring after flowering is over. More severe pruning will be required in mixed borders or where space is limited.

Propagation is simple: lift the plant in late winter and pull apart, replanting each rooted piece. As the lax stems often root naturally, when only a few plants are required these rooted pieces can be lifted for use. If large quantities are needed, take cuttings in late summer after new growth is complete. These are of pieces with four pairs of leaves with the lower pair removed to allow insertion into a sandy rooting mixture, and lined out in boxes or in a frame.

Polyanthus

Polyanthus is the latinised form of two Greek words *poly* and *anthos*, meaning 'many flowered' and was applied 400 years ago to any kind of *Primula* that had a multi-head of flowers. The first use of 'polyanthus' referring to a specific plant would seem to be in William Lucas's catalogue of 1677, in which both seeds and plants were offered for sale. In gardening books published earlier in the century there are names such as coloured cowslips, oxlips, paigles, arthritica and paralysis, with illustrations which might be the same as polyanthus, which they certainly resemble.

Although in the primrose the individual flowers appear to arise direct from the rootstock, they are in fact attached to a compressed stem which remains below ground. Very occasionally this stem will elongate, and it was from one or several of these freak primroses that the polyanthus may have developed. It is though, generally considered to be a hybrid between primrose (*Primula vulgaris*) and cowslip (*P. veris*). In nature, where these two plants are growing together hybrids do occur which, because they resemble the oxlip (*P. elatior*) are called 'false' or 'hybrid oxlip' (*P.X variabilis*). This was the plant which was collected at Great Wulver wood in 1650 by William How, and described by him as *Primula veris polyanthos*. The false oxlip, though, is always yellow, whereas the earliest polyanthus were red, sometimes purple. *Primula vulgaris* which is widespread in western Europe is replaced in Turkey by *P. vulgaris* ssp *sibthorpei* in which yellow as a flower colour is rare; shades mostly vary between red and purple. This plant was already being grown in England by 1640 for it appears in Parkinson's *Theatrum Botanicum* as 'Tradescant's purple Turkey primrose'. Hybrids have been recorded between this plant and the cowslip so it seems that this may have been the origin of the polyanthus. Whatever its origin, the polyanthus arose and was developed in England, for in other European countries it was known for almost a century as the English primula. Although its development had begun in the closing years of the seventeenth century it was in the following one that it was to become immensely popular, when its flower colours were of varying shades of velvety red or purple and those most prized were edged with silver or gold.

During the eighteenth century the polyanthus became a florists' flower. A florist at this time was not a person who made his living selling cut blooms but a gardener who specialised in growing many kinds of one or more sorts of flowers. These early florists formed clubs where information on cultivation was exchanged, and they organised floral feasts where plants in bloom were exhibited in competition. Floral feasts had begun in the seventeenth century and there is a record of one being held at Norwich as early as 1631. By the middle of the next century they were being held in most towns in England, Scotland and Ireland, often several times a year. Originally these had been social events for the gentry but artisans were later allowed to compete and were soon carrying off many of the prizes. The earliest plant to hold pride of place at these floral feasts was the auricula, but it was to be challenged later by the polyanthus. Auricula was the flower of the gentry who grew and displayed them in containers. These pots were housed on stages in wooden structures supporting rolled blinds made of thin slats of wood, which could be let down to provide protection: in winter to plants and containers from frost, and in spring to the blooms from heavy rain. It was the artisans who specialised in the cultivation of polyanthus in shady borders, and at flowering time these were lifted and put into pots for display. In the early years of the nineteenth century, floral feasts were replaced by the flower shows that we know today, when a much wider range of horticultural produce was displayed in competition from flower and kitchen garden, orchard and glasshouse.

As the floral feast declined in the last decade of the eighteenth century so did the cultivation of the polyanthus and it all but disappeared from gardens during the next 60 years. When it reappeared it was as a constituent in the new style of spring bedding. Now though, flowers were of self colours, mainly white or yellow, so it seems that breeding must have begun again but this time with *P.X variabilis,* the false oxlip. Coloured polyanthus were known at this time but their progeny was too variable and unreliable when raised from seed to be used for bedding. The next major development took place in the years after the Second World War, with the introduction of the Pacific strains from North America. These had very large flowers in a wide range of self colours which bred almost true from seed. While they became popular garden plants for spring display in countries with mild winters, in England they were too easily damaged by bad weather at flowering time. Eventually however, they were to become the most important of the commercial florists' spring flowers and it is as house plants that the largest number are sold today. Meanwhile English seedhouses had been developing their own strains and while flowers may be slightly smaller, there is the same range of colours as the Pacific strains they breed true and they are fully weather resistant. At present there is an interest in old fashioned flowers and the old gold laced polyanthus of 200 years ago have been rediscovered. Seeds of these are being offered for sale but the progeny is rather variable and there is a need for further breeding to produce purer lines.

Today polyanthus are grown as pot plants for home or cool glasshouse decoration or as bare-rooted plants to be used in the garden as fillers in a herbaceous border or island bed, or as ground cover in spring bedding. Although mixtures are mostly offered by garden centres, it is a group of the same colour flowers which makes most impact, except for the blues, which are too sombre on their own and need a contrast with a white or pale yellow polyanthus or spring flowering bulbs. Seed of these large-flowered polyanthus is rather expensive and some care is needed when sowing to ensure maximum success. Use a compost of equal parts of lime-free soil, sand and peat and sow the seed very thinly on the surface in a seed box or large pot, and just cover. Careful attention is needed with watering for if the soil becomes even slightly dry once the germination process has begun, the number of seedlings which appear can be small. Time of sowing depends on the size of plant required at flowering and the method by which they are to be grown. For the largest plants for bedding, the first sowing can be at the end of winter in gentle heat. When the seedlings are large enough to handle they can be lined out in a nursery bed being transferred to the position in which they are to flower in early autumn. For smaller bedding plants or if plants are to be grown in pots, sow seed in late spring and prick out when big enough to handle, putting one into a small pot using a compost of the same recipe. When these pots fill with roots, they can be potted on or they can be fed at two weekly intervals with a weak liquid feed. Pots should be provided with glasshouse or frame protection when frosts threaten; pick over plants, removing dead leaves and water carefully when required. When their flowers have faded plants can be divided and put out into a shady corner of the garden, and grown on throughout the summer and then used for planting out in early autumn.

Pomegranate

Pomegranate is a fruit that used to be popular, especially at Christmas, but which seems to be out of favour at the present time. The fruit, as big as a large apple, has a coronet of large brown sepals attached to a smooth leathery rind which is yellow or orange and often flushed with red or purple. Within the fruit is a mass of large white seeds, each of which is surrounded by an edible yellow jelly-like pulp. This pulp has been used for making syrups, one of which is called grenadine, alcoholic beverages and a jelly-like conserve. From the scarlet flowers a red dye has been produced and from the bark an extract which has been used for dyeing or colouring leather yellow. According to Gerard, the syrup was used as a cure for heartburn, prevented vomiting, strengthened the stomach and stopped bleeding internally or externally. From Parkinson's *Paradisus* comes: 'it is effective against ulcers of mouth and other parts of the body' and 'the rind do make the best sort of writing ink which is durable to the world's end'.

Pomegranate is derived from Norman French and means 'seedy' or 'grainy apple'. Gerard records that the Spanish word for pomegranate is *granata*, from which the city of Granada took its name because of the large number of pomegranates that grew in the neighbourhood. 'Granada' has been used as an alternative name, and so has 'grenadier'; the soldiers who bear this name are said to be so-called because the colour of their uniforms was the same as the flowers of the pomegranate. *Punica granatum* (the botanical name for pomegranate) came to Rome from Carthage; the Romans called the fruit *Malus* or *Pomum punicum,* apple of Carthage. 'Punic' as an adjective referred to Carthage, and this is one possible derivation of the generic name. Another is the Latin word *puniceus* which means 'reddish' or 'reddish purple', a reference to the colour of the ripe fruit. The specific epithet may be derived from the Spanish word for the fruit, but it could equally be from the Latin word *granatum* which is a seed. In Australia, a slang word for an Englishman is 'pommy' which is said to be a contraction of 'pomegranate'. Perhaps Australians saw a similarity between the rosy cheeks of the newly arrived immigrants and the flush on ripe fruit.

112

Pomegranates were known to all the ancient civilisations around the Mediterranean as well as those of India, Afghanistan and Persia. Theophrastus, who lived more than 300 years before Christ, mentioned that there were many kinds of pomegranate and Dioscorides in the first century AD recorded pink, red and white flowers. Although naturalised in many countries in southern Europe and North Africa, it is probable that the species originated from Persia. The pomegranate was brought into England by the Romans and after the decline of Roman influence survived in monastery gardens until the end of the Middle Ages when it came into the gardens of the gentry. William Turner wrote that it was growing at Syon House in 1548, and it was in Gerard's garden at Holborn in 1596. All the best known gardeners of the seventeenth century were growing it: Parkinson, Tradescant (father and son), Sir Thomas Hanmer, Rea, Evelyn and Walter Stonehouse, a Yorkshire cleric. Most considered the plant to be tender with recommendations that it be housed in winter. An exception was John Evelyn, the diarist, for in a letter which he wrote from his home at Sayes Court on 21st August 1668 to the Earl of Sandwich (the ambassador to the Spanish court) we read: 'I have always kept it exposed and the severest of our winters does it no prejudice; they will flower plentifully, but beare no fruit with us either kept in cases and in the respository, or set in ye open ayre at least very triflingly with ye greatest industry of stoves and other artifices'. In the seventeenth century pomegranates were grown for their flowers although in some summers ripe fruit was gathered. A number of types had been classified by this time: the barren, which referred to those with double flowers; and three qualities of fruit from the singles: sweet, sour and winey. Gardeners in the eighteenth century considered them more hardy and one reads that ripe fruit was gathered in most years from bushes planted against a south facing wall or on the outside of the kitchen chimney breast. In the last decade of the seventeenth century, a dwarf form arose in the West Indies and was introduced into England. This was in general cultivation by 1706 and called the 'American Pomegranate', described by all gardening authors as being tender. There is today a dwarf form which does not exceed 3ft (1m) which must be of a later introduction for it is definitely hardy. It can be raised from seed and is often treated as an annual as it flowers in its first year. While the dwarf pomegranate can be used for glasshouse decoration in summer or as a constituent of summer bedding, it can also be grown at the front of a shrub border.

Today the ordinary pomegranate, when grown in gardens, is treated as a flowering shrub for even in the mildest gardens, ripe fruit is only rarely produced and is much too sour for general use. It is surprisingly little seen and yet it produces its very striking flowers in late summer and autumn when there is a general scarcity of flowering shrubs. Occasionally in English gardens other colours besides orange and red can be seen, namely yellow or white of which there are both singles and doubles. In warmer countries there are shades of pink, salmon and bicolours.

Although it can be grown in a sunny shrub border, a longer flowering season results when it is planted against a south facing wall. Although in the wild it can make a small tree up to 20ft (6m), in English gardens it is unlikely to reach half this height and is more often treated as a medium sized shrub. Flowers are produced on current season's growth and some annual pruning is desirable in spring before new growth begins. This should consist of thinning out crowded, and thin shoots and shortening growth produced in the previous season.

   Cuttings taken of mature non-flowering growth in midsummer can be rooted under glass. Some success can be achieved by taking cuttings of bare current season's growth in winter and lining them out in the open ground.

Primrose

It is often thought that 'primrose' is derived from the Latin *prima rosa* which means 'first rose' (in earlier centuries, 'rose' was not as specific as it is today). The word, though, is derived from Norman French *primervole*, which had been corrupted by the fourteenth century to *primerole*, in which form it appears in Chaucer's *Miller's Tale*. By the sixteenth century it had arrived at the form we know today, for in Shakespeare's *Midsummer Night's Dream* we read:

In the wood where often you and I
Upon faint primrose-beds were wont to lie.

For a plant which has been for so long a universal favourite it has surprisingly few other names: there is only 'butter-rose', and although 'key flower' or 'ladies key' have been used, these are translations from the German and refer to legends where primroses were used to unlock secrets of buried treasure.

Primula vulgaris is widespread in western Europe from Denmark southwards to the Mediterranean and across into the mountains of North Africa. In Turkey and the Caucasus, the common primrose is replaced with *P. vulgaris* ssp *sibthorpei* whose flower colour ranges from pink to purple and where yellow is rare. Persia has *P. vulgaris* ssp *heterochroma* (sometimes considered a separate species), where the dominant flower colour is white although shades in the blue part of the spectrum are not uncommon. Finally confined to Mallorca is the sweetly scented white *P. vulgaris* ssp *balearica*.

Widespread throughout Britain, the common primrose favours a heavier soil containing or overlying limestone or chalk. Preferring light shade it is to be found at the edge of or under thin deciduous woodland, in copses at the foot of hedges and even in full sun in meadows where grass is short or lightly grazed. A herbaceous plant dying back to a short, rather stout rootstock, flowers, depending on the weather, can be produced as leaves begin to appear until fully developed over a period of about four months. Each bloom is borne on a thin stem which seems to rise directly from the rootstock although it is in fact attached to a stouter compressed stem which does not develop. While pale yellow with a hint of green is the most usual colour, white flowers can be found occasionally and in parts of Devon, Cornwall, Pembroke and Northumberland, there are colonies where flowers are pink or reddish. Careful examination of the flowers will show that there are two types: in one the stamens sit at the throat of the tube with the stigma out of sight below (thrum-eyed), while in the other the stigma protrudes through the stamens (pin-eyed). This is a device to ensure cross pollination; when there are plants with only thrum- or pin-eyed flowers, seed set can be poor.

The primrose was one of the earliest plants from the English countryside to be taken into gardens where by the sixteenth century it had become common. At that time a number of groups of flowers with curious floral structures were in fashion that were never again to be so. There were jack-in-the-greens, sometimes called jack-on-horseback, where the sepals had been replaced by miniature leaves so that they resembled a ruff around the flower. In hose-in-hose flowers, the calyx had become petaloid to suggest one flower inside another (in Tudor times it was the fashion for men to wear two pairs of stockings, one on top of the other; the understocking went up to the thighs, while the outer was turned down at the knee). In the final group the calyx had become inflated and was referred to as 'gally-gaskins', a kind of gaiter or sometimes pantaloons.

Gerard and Parkinson grew only three colours: yellow, green and white, but as both singles and doubles. The colour range was only extended with the introduction of *P. vulgaris* ssp *sibthorpei* said to have arrived in this country in 1638, which was described in *Theatrum Botanicum* of 1640 by John Parkinson as 'Tradescant's purple Turkey primrose'. With such a common name it might be thought that it was introduced into England by one of the John Tradescants, but this is not so; it was, however, distributed from their garden at Lambeth. John Rea in *Flora, Ceres and Pomona'* published in 1665 records: 'in the colour of the flowers there being almost twenty diversities of reds, some deep and others lighter from blood-red to pale pink colour, some of a blewish rose colour, sadder and paler, some brick colour others the colour of an old buff coat and some hair colour: all which varieties have been raised from seeds'. He mentions a double red, and purples and a blue form were being grown in

English gardens before the end of the century.

Even the beautiful primrose was used for more practical purposes than the decoration of a garden. Fritters or tansies were made from flowers fried in an egg batter. In spring fresh flowers were added to salads, while for other seasons the flowers were candied. In medicine, both primroses and cowslips were used for 'joynte-aches' and common names that were applied to either or both were 'arthritica' and 'paralysis'. According to William Coles in *Adam in Eden* (1658), 'The roots of primrose stamped and strained and the juyce snifted into the nose with a quill or such like, purgeth the brain and qualifieth the pain of the megrim'. A poultice of the leaves was used to extract thorns and splinters that were embedded beneath the skin.

The ancient Greeks considered the primrose to be a flower of melancholy, and Shakespeare more than once associated it with death. Taking but a single flower into the house brought bad luck. A more joyous association was its use in the many rituals carried out by young girls when they wanted to forsee whom they would marry. Moving towards more modern times there is Primrose Day, which is the anniversary of the death of Benjamin Disraeli whose favourite flower it had been.

During the eighteenth and nineteenth centuries the fashion for primroses in gardens fluctuated. The colour range during the period was extended and more doubles appeared with breeding to improve constitution and weather resistance. A new colour break followed the introduction of *P. vulgaris* ssp *heterochroma* in 1882 and in 1890 G. F. Wilson reintroduced a blue primrose more than two hundred years after it had first appeared. Wilson's primrose, although it was available in sufficient quantities by the first decade of the twentieth century for use in spring bedding, did not survive very long for it, too, disappeared from cultivation. After the Second World War breeding in the United States produced strains with large flowers that bred true, and amongst these was a true blue. One wonders if future breeding with *P. vulgaris* ssp *balearica* will introduce strongly fragrant primroses.

As primroses transplant readily, even when in full flower, they have been uprooted from the countryside in such numbers that in some places where they were once common, they are now rare. The wild primrose seems out of place in a well managed suburban garden and looks most at home when planted in a wild garden.

Local enthusiasts who care for road verges and motorway strips may plant primroses in these areas or include its seed with those of other wild flowers in grass mixtures when they come to grass down these banks. The large modern hybrids are used mainly for spring bedding or perhaps as fillers in herbaceous borders or island beds. Just as modern polyanthus are important pot plants for decorating the home, so too are the coloured primroses, but on a smaller scale.

An interest in growing or collecting together cvs of old-fashioned garden flowers has resulted in old gardens and specialist nurseries being scoured in the search for them. Amongst the finds are old doubles which have been raised over a period of almost 400 years. Unfortunately these are of weak constitution, and unless one has a favourable garden, they are difficult to keep. They are best grown in isolation in a slightly shady position, in a heavier soil that contains organic matter and some lime and which does not dry out in summer.

When using primroses in spring bedding, make an underplanting of one colour only, which is much more effective than using mixed colours. Grow through them early flowering bulbs that do not grow too high, e.g. garden hyacinths, Tenby daffodils or one of the cvs of *Tulipa kaufmanniana*. The blues are too sombre on their own and need light coloured bulb flowers for contrast; alternatively interplant with a white or pale yellow cv of primrose.

Rather than dig up wild primroses from the countryside, plants for the garden or even for beautifying road verges can be raised from seed now offered for sale by a few of the smaller seed firms. Seed of these and the modern hybrids which are to be used in bedding should be sown in containers on the firmed surface of a compost made up of equal parts of lime-free soil, sand and peat and just covered. Careful watering is needed, for if the soil becomes slightly dry during the germination process, very few seedlings will appear. Timing will depend on the size of plants required and the way in which they are to be grown. For the largest plants for use in bedding the first sowing will be made in early spring, while for smaller plants or those to be grown to flower in pots, sowing can be delayed until the very end of spring. Depending on how thickly the seed has been sown, some pricking out may well be necessary when the seedlings are large enough, if they have been sown thinly, the seedlings can be either potted from the seed container or lined out in nursery beds to be grown on for transplanting in the autumn. Pots should be kept in a shady part of the garden, and if they fill with roots, they can be potted on; if they are to be retained in their first pots until flowering, apply dilute liquid feed at two weekly intervals. Protect the pots in a cold frame or glasshouse when the frosts arrive. When flower beds are cleared in readiness for planting summer bedding, the primroses can be divided up and each rooted piece replanted in a nursery bed. Named cvs, whether single or double, can be increased by division after flowering with the rooted pieces either potted or replanted into well prepared soil.

Privet

'Privet' refers to two quite different species of the genus *Ligustrum;* originally it was used for the European *L. vulgare* but it was transferred to, or came to include the Japanese *L. ovalifolium* when it was introduced into Europe during the nineteenth century. Today *L. vulgare* may be called 'common privet', while *L. ovalifolium* is just 'privet', 'oval-leafed privet', 'Japanese privet' and in North America, 'Californian privet'.

Ligustrum vulgare extends from southern Scandinavia to the Mediterranean and from Britain across to Russia. It makes a large shrub or small tree to 15ft (4m). Depending on how cold winters are it can be partially evergreen or completely deciduous. There are opposite leaves which are narrowly lance-shaped, tapering to a point, which are up to ¾in. (18mm) wide. Produced at the apex of previous year's growth on main stems or side shoots are panicles of dull white or cream flowers; these are scented, but many people find this fragrance repellent. Flowers are followed by bunches of round or oval dull black fruits which last well into the winter. In *Trees and Shrubs Hardy in the British Isles,* Bean lists a naturally occurring variety *italicum,* which is described as being more regularly evergreen than these other type; there is mention also of cvs with variegated yellow leaves and others in which there are berries that are green, yellow or white.

L. *ovalifolium* is confined to Japan, and makes a large shrub or tree up to 16ft (5m) with broader leaves than the former (up to 1¼in. (32mm) and with rounded tips. Flowers are similar in form and colour and there is the same unpleasant scent; berries are always globose and of a shining black. There are two variegated cvs; in one, margins are banded with white, and in the other with yellow. It would seem that there are several forms of golden privet with differing widths of coloured margin, intensity of colour and degree of stability of colour. Hedges can be seen where a number of bushes have reverted to green and these, being stronger of growth, produce an uneven and blotchy appearance.

The common privet was brought into European gardens at least 500 years ago when it was used for making hedges. The Romans had used privet for topiary some 2000 years ago but this fashion of clipping bushes into often bizarre shapes did not reappear in Europe until the sixteenth century. While it was especially fashionable in Holland, where entire gardens were devoted to the art, it came into England on a more restricted scale with topiary subjects being included in parterres. There is a fine topiary garden at Levens Hall in Cumbria which dates from the early years of the eighteenth century. Because common privet is not long lived, there are no old topiary examples of this shrub extant; the oldest are of box or yew. Topiary went out of fashion in the grand gardens in the eighteenth century when landscape became informal, to come back in the following century when formality returned. Today it is too demanding of labour to be practised on a large scale, but it remains as popular as ever in cottage gardens.

During the sixteenth and seventeenth centuries plants had to be useful in a garden. Although common privet is native in Britain, suprisingly few uses have been found for it. A dye was made from its berries, which was used as an ink or for colouring wine. Poultices made with the leaves were used to reduce swellings and inflammation. In Gerard's *Herbal* can be read: 'leaves of privet do cure ulcers of the mouth or throat being gargarified with iuyce or decoction thereof'. In the nineteenth and early twentieth centuries common privet was used by nurserymen as an understock on which cvs of lilac were grafted. If grafting of lilac has to be carried out, privet is better as a stock than the suckers of or the seedlings of lilac, for if suckering of a stock does take place in the garden, privet shoots are easily recognised and can be removed.

Common privet, which had been used from earliest times for hedging, tended to be replaced in the eighteenth century by the Italian, which was more evergreen. According to Batty Langley in *New Principles of Gardening* (1727), 'This sort of Privet was brought from Italy by the ingenious Mr Balle of Kensington which in the Italian: is called Olivetta because of its leaves which are not unlike those of the Olive'. Italian privet was being offered for sale by John and George Telford of York in their catalogue of 1775 at two pence each, and a striped form at one penny. In 1833, F. Mackie of Norwich had evergreen Italian privet at 1½–2ft. (450–600mm) at 8/- (40p) per 100. He was offering Chinese privet at 12/-(60p) a dozen, a high price for those days; while this may be the Japanese privet it is more likely to have been *L. lucidum* which had arrived in England in 1769.

L. ovalifolium arrived in England soon after the start of the Industrial Revolution when people were moving into towns and cities, which expanded rapidly to accommodate them. This coincided with an upsurge of the middle classes, for whom larger houses were provided, with terraces or cottages for the working class. Gardens were now standard with houses of whatever size and all were enclosed to provide privacy. The choice of plant material for the hedges would be governed by cost, and privet, being quickly and easily raised, was the cheapest. There was the added advantage of its ability to grow in any kind of soil: acid or alkaline, sand or clay, dry or wet; in full sun or shade; moreover it established quickly, would withstand regular and frequent clippings and was tolerant of the severe atmospheric pollution which resulted from fumes belching out from coal fires. By the end of the century though, many garden writers were beginning to condemn privet hedges. William Robinson carried out a diatribe against its planting, commenting even at his least vitriolic, that it was the meanest of all shrubs and not worth having anywhere in a garden. This dislike of privet has afflicted almost all writers even to the present day: they all ask their readers not to make hedges or privet. Yet in spite of their denigration, gardeners still use privet more than any other plant for hedges because of its cheapness and its good points, which outweigh the bad. Both kinds of privet have some attraction when planted in any of their forms as a free-standing shrub left untrimmed, for foliage, flower or fruit.

'Privet' is possibly an alternative spelling or corruption of 'private', for privet from the earliest days has been used to provide seclusion and to hide unsightly features. It has been suggested that it acquired this name because it was used to hide privies before there was indoor sanitation. An old English name was 'prim' or 'prim print' which, it is assumed referred to the neatness of a newly trimmed hedge. 'Mock privet' has been used as an alternative name for lilac (*Syringa vulgaris*), a buckthorn (*Rhamnus alaternus*) and species of *Phillyrea*.

A hedge, once planted, is expected to remain in good condition for many decades, so thorough preparation is needed. Mark out a strip of ground a yard/metre wide and double dig, breaking up the second spit and incorporating in it as much organic matter as possible. Allow to settle and tread so that the ground is evenly firm. If the soil sits proud, remove the surplus and several more inches/millimetres so as to form a shallow trench. Buy bare-rooted plants during winter and plant a single row 12–18in. (300–450mm) apart. Following planting cut hard back to encourage branching from ground level. During the first summer, watering in dry weather will aid establishment and encourage strong growth. In the following three winters, or until the required height has been reached, reduce new growth by half.

Privet is strong growing, producing long annual shoots which if left or only lightly trimmed make a thin base. Sides of the hedge should be trimmed so that they slope from a broad base to a narrower top. This follows the natural development of any shrub and ensures that a hedge remains well clothed to its base; if this becomes thin or bare it is impossible to reclothe without drastic action. A tidy gardener may want neat hedges at all times and this will necessitate trimming at least at two weekly intervals. For the gardener with only limited time to spend in his garden, one trimming is enough if carried out in midsummer when new growth is complete and is beginning to mature. Privet is a greedy shrub, and annual feeding is beneficial, with a dressing of a general fertiliser at 2 ounces to each yard of run (68 grams per metre) in late winter.

Propagation is very easy using hardwood cuttings taken in winter. These are taken from annual growth of an unpruned shrub and cut into lengths 8–10in. (200–250mm) which are inserted to two-thirds of their length into a slit trench into which is put some coarse sand, and then thoroughly firmed by the heels. Rooted cuttings can be lifted twelve months later.

Rosemary

Rosemary is a plant that has been attributed to the Virgin Mary. *Rosmarinus*, its generic name, is derived from two Latin words: *ros* meaning 'dew' and *marinus* suggesting a maritime association, and in translation it has become 'sea dew'; *officinalis*, its specific epithet, means 'of use to man'. The Greek word for rosemary is *libanotis;* from this word has been derived *labanou* which means 'frankincense', and rosemary has been used as a substitute for incense in church rituals.

In English gardens it is a shrub, and in the 8th edition of Bean's *Trees and Shrubs Hardy in the British Isles* (1980) it is said to make a bush 6–7ft (2–2.3m) high; in *Adam in Eden* (1657) William Coles writes of it reaching 3–4 cubits (1 cubit = 22 inches or 550mm), but in nature it can make a small tree with a trunk of 10ft (3m) which has a shaggy bark. It is widespread in southern Europe amongst the maquis and its fragrance on hot summer days can be smelt for long distances: John Evelyn reported its fragrance as being discernable 30 leagues seaward of the Spanish coast.

One of the best known quotations from Shakespeare's Hamlet is: 'There's rosemary, that's for remembrance' but its association with memory goes back much further in time. Students in ancient Greece used to wear wreathes of rosemary on their heads when studying or 'swotting' for examinations. It has had a long association with death in many European countries; as an indication of and to retain a memory of the deceased. A sprig was put into the hands of a corpse in his coffin, whilst branches were carried by mourners in funeral processions and were thrown into the grave before it was filled. It was also used for much more joyful occasions like weddings. Sprays of rosemary which had been gilded were worn or carried by the groom or groomsmen and a chaplet of rosemary was worn by the bride or carried in her bouquet, or was in the posies of her bridesmaids. Cuttings taken from the wedding adornments were inserted into the newly weds' garden and if these rooted and thrived, then the woman would be master of the home. It was used to decorate the home at Christmas to indicate amity, joy and happy memories. Planting of rosemary in gardens gave protection against the evil eye and it was a plant dedicated to fairies; in Portugal it is called the 'elfin plant'. When gardening was taken up by the gentry to adorn the exteriors of their houses at the end of the Middle Ages, rosemary was considered essential planting, first in knot gardens and later in parterres as edging for or contents of the patterned beds. Rosemary had been trained against the wall at Hampton Court in the sixteenth century and Sir Thomas More had recommended extensive plantings in a garden for bees.

In the sixteenth and seventeenth centuries it was used as a strewing herb to sweeten the atmosphere in parlours and bedrooms in the same way as we would use deodorants today. Just as we use, or did use, mothballs, 400 years ago rosemary was added to chests of linen to keep away moths and one of its names, 'guardrobe', shows that this is how it was used in France; there is also a word with the same meaning in Spanish: *guardalobo*. At this time ladies and gentlemen too, when venturing into the streets carried posies of flowers and fragrant herbs, including rosemary, at which they sniffed – to make the nose gay by disguising the foul smells of the streets; nosegays were also thought to give protection against plague. Leaves and flowers steeped in water produced an infusion that was used for washing or bathing the body to cleanse and clear the skin and remove unpleasant smells. Ground charcoal made from wood of rosemary was used to clean teeth, strengthen gums, cure ulcers of the mouth and to sweeten the breath. Dried leaves on their own or mixed with tobacco and smoked not only cured asthma but 'helpeth them that have any cough, tiffick or consumption'. Rosemary was effective against disorders of the head; as a cure for giddiness, loss of speech, palsy, headaches and cold in the head, and was a stimulant to the memory. In the kitchen it was added as a flavouring to soups and pottage, to stuffing for poultry, game and meats and in the preparation of a calf's or boar's head. Fresh flowers were added to salads, made into pickles or when candied, eaten as comfits.

In the garden today it is appreciated primarily for its fragrant leaves. These can be narrow or broad and vary from the darkest green to grey and shades of blue. The gilded rosemary, which has been known for at least 400 years, is still to be found in a few gardens and nurseries. This may have been used in wedding celebrations although it is more likely that sprigs were gilded by dipping into gold paint. It is an unattractive plant for its blotchy yellowing suggests infection by a disease or severe infestation by some pest (the yellowness is in fact virus-induced). This colouring is not constant but can disappear completely at certain times of the year. Many old garden books mention a silver striped rosemary, but this seems to be lost to cultivation. Philip Miller writes of it as being tender and rare in 1768, for almost all plants had been killed in the severe winter of 1740. Flower colour is most usually a pale lavender but there is a form described as 'white', although this is not a clean colour. There are various shades of pink, of which the best is probably Majorca Pink. A number of recently introduced forms, all of which seem to be low growing, have much larger flowers which are of a deeper almost sky blue and are suprisingly hardy; one of these is Beneden Blue, introduced by Captain Collingwood Ingram and named after his house. For the rock garden there is a carpeting form: the variety *prostrata*, which can with age build up into a low mound; it is especially effective when planted at the top of a wall or large rock where its stems can cascade downwards.

Rosemary is likely to be damaged by exceptionally cold weather and such damage will be all the more severe following a wet summer or autumn when wood does not ripen properly. Plant always in a warm sunny place in a garden protected from cold winds, in full sun and in a rather poor soil which contains lime. Ideally rosemary should be positioned near to a path or window where sprigs can be plucked for sniffing, and to make it easier to gather for the kitchen The narrow (Miss) Jessup's Upright can be planted on either side of a door to frame it, or it is useful for making a hedge to divide up a garden. Although one of the hardier forms, its flowers have little merit and when a flowering hedge is wanted, then use Tuscan Blue, although this is not as cold resistant. Flowering which occurs over much of the year tends to come in flushes, with that of spring being the best. After this spring flush, preferably before new growth has begun, carry out any pruning which may be necessary and trim to shape, using sharp garden shears. Bushes which have become overgrown, untidy or have been winter damaged, can be cut back hard with secateurs at this time.

Cuttings taken of mature growth in late summer are easy to root with some protection. Rooted cuttings should be kept in a cold frame or glasshouse for spring planting after the danger of frost has gone.

Rose of Sharon

Of the many names applied to this plant over the last three hundred years, that of 'rose of sharon' is the most puzzling.

While *Rosa phoenicea* has been proposed for the rose of sharon in the Bible, it is now generally accepted that this common name was not applied to what we understand as a rose today. It is now thought that the plant was a kind of bulb, and a number have been put forward as possible contenders: a crocus, *Tulipa montana*, *T. sharonensis*, *Lilium candidum* and *Narcissus tazzeta*. In more recent times, 'rose of sharon' has been used for *Hibiscus syriacus*, although what most gardeners understand by this common name today is *Hypericum calycinum*. The first use of 'rose of sharon' for this species of *Hypericum* seems to have been in 1864 in *British Garden Botany* by L. Grindon. No reason is given for this new name nor for 'Aaron's beard', another common name which came into use at about the same time; both have continued to be used as alternative names.

Hypericum calycinum, native to European Turkey and Bulgaria is now widespread throughout much of Europe due to escapes from cultivation. It was introduced into England from Byzantium by Sir George Wheeler in 1676 while he was on the grand tour after coming down from Oxford. He sent seed to Robert Morison, the first professor of botany at Oxford, and plants were growing in the botanic garden of that city before the end of the century. It soon became widely grown in gardens and by 1775 was being offered in the catalogue of John and George Telford, nurserymen of York, at 2d. each. In Ireland it had escaped from cultivation, for in gardening and botanical books of the nineteenth century, there are frequent references to it being an Irish native plant. For at least a century after its introduction it was known as 'Sir George Wheeler's tutsan'. 'Tutsan' and 'St John's Wort' are both general names for all species of *Hypericum* and two other common names for *H. calycinum* were: 'large flowered tutsan' and 'large flowered St. John's Wort'. The genus *Hypericum* is dedicated to Saint John the Baptist and on his Saint's day, 24th June, the church was decorated with tutsan flowers or they were worn or carried by members of the congregation. Early christians had taken over celebrations from pagan deities and as 24th June coincided with the summer solstice, flowers of various *Hypericum* species had been used in these pagan rites; two other common names may be derived from these uses: 'summer sun' and 'terrestrial sun'. Even after christianity had come to Europe, for many centuries there were fears from peasants about demons and any species of *Hypericum* was referred to as *fuga daemonium* because sprigs would put demons to flight; plants growing in a garden provided protection against witches, warlocks, the evil eye and strikes by lightning.

'Tutsan' is derived from two French words *tout* and *sain* and means 'to cure' or 'heal all', an indication that all native species as well as those from other countries were much used in medicine. Oil of St. John's Wort was used to cure old sores, ulcers, green internal and external wounds, while an infusion stayed internal bleeding and prevented the vomiting of blood. As a poultice it eased the pain of sciatica and muscular strain and was used for convulsions and to purge choleric humours.

Rose of sharon is one of the easiest shrubs to grow in a garden. Of suckering habit, it is low growing and spreading, about 18in. (450mm) high and perhaps 3ft (1m) across. When winters are mild, leaves are evergreen, but with lower temperatures may be semi-evergreen or completely deciduous; leaves, on arching stems, are arranged in opposite pairs and are broadly oval, upto 2in. (50mm) long. Flowers are produced terminally, each of which can be 3in. (75mm) in diameter and made up of five golden yellow petals around a prominent boss of stamens.

Indifferent to soil, rose of sharon will succeed whether it is acid or alkaline, wet or dry, and grows well in full sun or shade, but flowering can be poor in low light. Most often it is planted in groups at the front of a shrub border. As flowers are produced on current season's growth, plants will be easier to manage by cutting back to ground level at the end of winter; this will produce larger flowers that are more easily seen. With this same treatment it can be used in the front of a herbaceous border or island bed. Today though, its main use is as ground cover and it is especially useful for steep, sunny bank; when used for ground cover no pruning would be necessary.

It is just as easy to increase as it is to grow. When only a few plants are required, an established clump can be lifted when dormant, the top cut off and the plant pulled to pieces, each piece with roots being replanted. For larger quantities, summer cuttings are easy to root when there is some protection. Those gardeners who have neither frames nor a glasshouse can use hardwood cuttings in winter which are rooted in the open ground. After pruning, cut current season's growth into pieces 4–6in. (100–150mm) in length and push into the ground so that their tips just protrude. Where soil is heavy, take out a slit trench, work in some sand at the bottom and then line out the cuttings to the same depth. Irrespective of how the cuttings are inserted, they should be thoroughly firmed with the feet.

Rue

Ruta graveolens is a low, compact, rounded bush with upright stems, woody at the base which can reach 3ft (1m). It is an evergreen whose fetid grey or blue-green compound leaves are alternately arranged, with the basal pair of leaflets three-lobed. In late summer, a branched inflorescence is produced terminally. Each flower, about ¾in. (18mm) across is made up of four petals with finely toothed edges of a dull light yellow in which there is a tinge of green. Following pollination, which seems to be carried out by flies, dry capsules are produced containing quite large, dark, almost black, shiny seeds. A native of many countries of southern Europe along the Mediterranean, it is found growing amongst rocks on dry limestone hillsides often making up part of the maquis.

It has been cultivated since early times, which accounts for a multitude of names in French, German, Italian and Spanish. The Latin *Ruta* and its English derivation, 'rue', refer to the bitterness of the leaves, and *graveolens* means strongly smelling. Some of the other English names are: 'common rue', 'garden rue', 'herb-of-repentence', 'herb-grace', 'ave-grace' and 'countryman's treacle'.

Although it is to be found in most herb gardens today it is little used either medicinally or in cooking. In the past it has been used to flavour sauces, meats and beverages and it is said to be a constituent of grappa. It was used to flavour vinegar, and leaves and immature fruits have been made into pickles. In a French gourmet's book there is mention of new leaves, finely chopped, being spread between slices of brown bread.

Medicinally, rue is a narcotic and stimulant usually used as 'oil of rue'. Modern research is once again turning to plants for curative extracts, and in rue is a substance which has proved beneficial in the treatment of high blood pressure. In times gone by it has been used for a number of ailments. All old herbals make mention of its use in bathing eyes to relieve tiredness and soreness, to restore their sparkle and to improve failing eyesight in the elderly. Taken internally it was used for such diverse ailments as headaches, sciatica, coughs, colic, worms, gout and bleeding of the nose. It may be that rue was used as a placebo for cures are meant to be unpleasant, and the more vile the taste, the more effective, would be its cure. Rue has been considered as a counter-poison for providing protection against the toxins in the stings of serpents, scorpions, toads, spiders, wasps and hornets. Sprigs have been hung up in a room to keep away flies and an infusion of leaves in water has been sprinkled around the house to kill fleas. Nosegays, which were carried by ladies and gentlemen too, when they ventured forth into the stinking streets of towns and cities in sixteenth and seventeenth century England, would contain rue; besides helping to disguise these foul smells, nosegays were considered to give protection against plague, and the more rue they contained, the better was the protection. Fantasy was never far removed from fact 400 years ago, and amongst the non-medical myths or legends one can read that rue gave protection against the evil eye; it was possible to expose a woman who was thought to be a witch (how is not recorded) and if a gun flint was boiled in a mixture of rue and vervain (*Verbena officinalis*), the bullet always found its target.

Rue is a gross feeder, needing a well drained, rich soil containing lime and to be planted in full sun. Although surprisingly hardy in dry winters, it is more prone to damage when the winters are wet. After a wet winter bushes can look bedraggled and may be damaged. Some pruning is beneficial if carried out just before new growth begins, when winter damage is removed and trimming takes place to produce a neater and tidier bush. Pruning in high summer when temperatures are high should be avoided, for many people are sensitive to rue sap, which can cause a painful rash or blisters on exposed skin. Rue should be considered as short lived, to be replaced at frequent intervals, retaining only as long as the bush remains neat, tidy and well clothed with leaves. Cuttings taken of non-flowering shoots in summer are easy to root if provided with some protection. Tradition has it that rue grows better when cuttings are stolen and this excuse is extended to many plants by lightfingered gardeners when they plunder gardens that they are visiting.

    In recent years, rue has escaped the confines of the herb garden and has come to be used in the flower garden with other kinds of foliage plants. It is useful for its blue foliage in bedding or when used in groups in island beds or herbaceous borders, and it provides summer interest if planted at the front of a shrub border. The cv Jackman's Blue in which the foliage is the bluest of blue-green has almost entirely replaced ordinary rue, for it is more compact and brighter in colour; it seems to come true from seed. There is a rather unpleasant variegated form which appeals to some people as a novelty, but this is untidy of growth and the white patterning of the leaves is not very strong.

Saffron

Saffron whose botanical name is *Crocus sativus*, is derived from the Arabic and means 'yellow' the same meaning as *crocus* in Greek, *sativus* comes from the Latin, meaning 'cultivated'. Originally 'saffron' had referred to the one plant, but during the sixteenth and seventeenth centuries it became a general name for all species of *Crocus*. Somewhat confusingly, 'meadow saffron' came to be used for all species of *Colchicum,* a genus of the Lily family, while *Crocus* belong to the Iris family. Today 'meadow saffron' is intended to refer to *Colchicum autumnale,* and all other species of this genus are referred to as 'autumn crocuses'.

Crocus sativus must be amongst the oldest of all cultivated plants for it was known to all the ancient European civilisations and its cultivation had spread to those of Persia and India. It is shown on a vase painting from ancient Crete, dated about 1500 BC. During its long period of cultivation it has come to be so widely grown in all temperate regions of the world that escapes from cultivation have become widely naturalised. Today saffron is sterile, which suggests that sometime in its history some superior form which had an extra large stigma had been selected for cultivation. It is from the stigma that commercial saffron is produced by drying; 4300 flowers are required to prepare just one ounce of saffron. Brian Mathew in his book *The Crocus* considers that saffron is a selection from *Crocus cartwrightianus,* a species that occurs in Greece and some of the adjacent islands. Saffron figures in the Greek herbal of Dioscorides, as a woodcut which was prepared in Byzantium in 512 AD. This book was to form the basis of medicine for the next one and a half millenia not only in Europe but throughout much of Asia. Mention in this book of where saffron was thought to grow shows that 1500 years ago *C. cartwrightianus* had already become naturalised outside its area of natural distribution. All that time ago saffron was much used in medicine and cookery and because of the large number of flowers needed for its preparation it has always been costly. In his book Dioscorides complained about merchants who adulterated saffron to boost profits. A thousand years later, English saffron would always find a ready market in Europe for it had the reputation of being pure and unadulterated.

It was the Romans who introduced saffron to England but it was not until more settled times following the Norman invasion that it came to be grown commercially, and it was to found the fortunes of the town which came to be known as Saffron Walden. Dioscorides had written that saffron stirred up venerie, assuaged inflammations and was used against earache. According to William Coles in *Adam in Eden* of 1657, 'It is very profitable for, the Head, Stomach, Spleen, Bladder, Womb, Animal Vitall Spirits and is useful in old diseases of the Braine and Nerves and quickens the memories and senses'. Because of its yellow colouring it was used to cure by signature jaundice. Amongst other ailments for which it effected a cure were measles, pleurisy, plague, smallpox and consumption. All herbalists of the seventeenth century warned that taking too much saffron could cause death. In addition to its uses in medicine it was used as a colouring agent and for flavouring; from Gerard's *Herbal:* 'The chives steeped in water serve to illumine (as we say) limne pictures and imagerie as also to colour sundry meat and confections; it is with good success given to procure bodily lust'. Today it is used in the preparation of Spanish rice dishes, French *bouillabaisse* and West of England saffron cakes.

Tropaeolum, Majus cultivars

Modern Primrose cultivars

Crocus sativus is a corm which is dormant in summer, coming into growth towards the end of that season or in early autumn with flowers appearing first, to be followed by the leaves which remain green throughout the winter and die back in late spring. In late medieval times, saffron was grown not only as a commercial crop but also in gardens for its beautiful flowers. It was the first crocus which had been brought into cultivation and it was considered of special value, for it came into flower when other summer blooms were fading. From the earliest days of gardening, bulbs had been much sought after and this fashion continued unabated to the present day, although it probably reached a peak in the second half of the nineteenth century. It was at this time that nurserymen and wealthy amateurs were commissioning collectors to send back bulbs from southern Europe and Asia Minor. This period saw the arrival of many species of crocus new to science, and the reintroduction of species which had been introduced centuries earlier but which had failed to establish. Saffron retained its place in gardens until it came to be superseded by other, more spectacular species which bloomed at the same season. It was during the late nineteenth century that the demand and commercial production of saffron declined following the introduction of more modern medicines and cheaper artificial colourings. Today its use in cooking is minimal, and the limited demand is supplied by imports from the warmer countries of Europe. In recent years, with the greater interest in the cultivation and use of herbs, the cultivation of saffron has had a minor revival; it has also been sought by the bulb enthusiast who has an interest in *Crocus* for its beautiful flowers.

Plant the corms 4in. (100mm) deep in summer or as soon as corms become available, in a well drained soil that has been thoroughly prepared, with organic matter incorporated. Flowers will quickly follow planting with leaves sometimes developing at the same time, but usually after the flowers have faded. Corms may be containerised for display in an alpine house. Using a compost of equal parts soil, peat and sand, put 2–3in. (50–75mm) of the mixture into a pan, place the corms close together and then cover with compost. Do not water until the leaves begin to appear, increasing the amount of water as they expand. Continue to water until the leaves begin to yellow and then gradually reduce watering but never allow the soil to become dust dry. When fully dormant, the bulbs can be taken out of their container and graded, with the largest being used for next year's flowering and the smaller ones grown on until they reach flowering size. Corms in the open ground are lifted every three or four years, pulled apart, graded and the largest replanted for flowering, while the smaller sizes are grown on in a nursery until they reach flowering size.

Sage

Originally 'sage' was the common name for *Salvia officinalis*, but now, used with an adjective it has become a name for all species of the genus so 'common' has been added to distinguish this variety from all the others. The common sage, a fragrant evergreen small shrub of southern Europe, was known and cultivated by all the ancient civilisations of the Mediterranean. In the first century AD, Dioscorides, a Greek physician, had written a book, *Materia Medica,* which was to guide herbalists for the next 1500 years; about sage he had written that an infusion could be used to dye the hair black and that it was a wound herb, blood stauncher and a cleanser of ulcers. In about 840 AD a monk of St Galle in what is now Switzerland, Walafrid Strabo, had written a book of poems called *Hortulus* about garden plants; of sage he wrote:

There in the front glows sage, sweetly scented
It deserves to grow green forever, enjoying perpetual youth
For it is rich in virtue and good to mix a potion
Of proven use for many a human ailment.
But within itself is the germ of civil war
For unless the new growth is cut away, it turns
Savagely upon its parent and chokes to death
The old stems in bitter jealousy.

(The last 4 lines refer to the need for regular pruning).

Salvia is derived from the Latin word *salvus,* which means 'safe', 'well' or 'sound', referring to the healing properties of the plant. In the sixteenth century it was a universal panacea. Gerard mentions many ailments that sage was used to cure, including:

Sage is singularly good for the head and braine, it quickeneth the senses and memory, strengtheneth the sinews, restoreth health to those that hath the palsie upon a moist cause, taketh away shaking and trembling members and being put into the nostrils, it draweth thin phlegme out of the head. It is likewise commended against the spitting of blood, the cough and paines of the side and the biting of serpents and there are many more.

In *Paradisis in Sole,* Parkinson repeats the cures listed by Gerard but also gives some culinary uses:

The kitchen use is either to boyle it with a calves head and being minced to put with braines, vinegar and pepper and to serve an ordinary sauce therunto; or beaten and juiced rather than minced as manie doe, is put to a roasted pigs braines with currans for sauce therewith. It is in small quantity in regard to the strong taste of veale when they are forced or stuffed therewith and roasted which they call ollives.

Sage ale, an infusion of leaves in beer; was advocated to improve health in men while for ladies it was sage tea, where the infusion was in hot water. Another remark made by Parkinson was 'sage is used of many in the moneth of May feeding with butter and parsley and is held of most to induce healthe of mans body'. Many other herbalists emphasised that sage was most efficacious when taken in May; no doubt in this month, just before flowers are produced, the leaves contain their highest content of aromatic oils. An old Arabian proverb makes the same point:

He that would live of aye
Must eat Sage in May.

John Evelyn, the diarist in similar vein makes this cynical comment:

'Tis a plant indeed with so many and wonderful properties that the evidence of it, is said to render man immortal'.

Today sage is probably the most widely grown of all herbs. It is much used in forcemeat for stuffing chickens, fowl, turkey and rolled mutton. It is used in the preparation of certain kinds of sausages and in sage Derby cheese. Fresh leaves may be added to a salad, but because of its strong taste it may be enough to just rub the inside of a salad bowl. It may be used to flavour soups, sauces and egg dishes. Probably there are no uses in medicine today although it was used for whitening teeth and to strengthen gums, long after the introduction of toothpaste.

Although in earlier centuries sage was grown for practical purposes, its ornamental value was not overlooked. In 1665, John Rea had written in his book *Flora, Ceres and Pomona*, 'Sage is of many sorts but those fitteth for this place (the flower garden) are the variegated great sage, the one marked white, the other with yellow and the small sweet sage; the variegated are common but the small more rare. There are several sort of the small sage but that here intended is a small tender plant of a musky scent far excelling all others'. In the seventeenth century, besides the small sage mentioned by Rea, there was, in addition to the ordinary green, the red sage whose virtues were considered greater than the green but less than the small. In the list of forms which appears in *The Gardener's Dictionary* of 1731 Philip Miller has: common green, green with variegated leaf, red, red with variegated leaf and the lesser. Today sage has escaped from the confines of the herb or vegetable garden and is coming to be grown more and more as an ornamental plant; there are two groups; one with attractive flowers and the other with ornamental foliage. Flowers are produced at the end of spring or the beginning of summer in terminal spikes which are mostly of a pale lavender, but there is a range of colours between blue and red. Nearest to a pure light blue is the large flowered Grandiflora. In Rubriflora the flowers are of dull red with a touch of mauve or purple and in Albiflora the flowers are of a good clean white. Spectacular as the flowers are, their display is of short duration – rarely more than three weeks.

Within the kinds grown for their foliage, there is a considerable variation in the number of flowers each produces; some flower freely, others sparsely and a few rarely or not at all. Of all the kinds grown in gardens today it is doubtful if any are really new. In the green sage, colour can vary from mid green to shades of grey, some of which are bluish. Just as there is variation in colour, so there is in leaf-shape: in Latifolia leaves are only twice as long as they are broad, whereas in Salicifolia the length is seven times the breadth; Crispa has crimped or crinkled leaf margins. In Aurea the leaf is completely yellow, but there seems to be more than one form under this name, varying from a faint yellowish green in colour to a good clear yellow. In general the colour is strongest in full sunshine but some kinds burn badly, especially when the soil is dry. Purpurascans, the red sage, also has many forms: there is variation in intensity of colour, which can be stronger at certain seasons, with some kinds flowering freely and others not at all. From time to time the red sage sports and produces variegated shoots, most often in the form of uneven blotching, which is unstable and reverts back to type no matter how frequently the plain red shoots are removed. There seems to have been a red with a white margin, but it is not known whether this still exists. In seventeenth and eighteenth century lists, a green with a variegated leaf appears, but this too seems to have been lost. The form which today is called Tricolor may be a sport of either of the two kinds previously mentioned, for there is a white margin to the leaf and the entire leaf is overlaid with purplish pink. This is the painted sage of the seventeenth century, which today has a weak constitution, is the most tender and can never be relied upon to survive a winter, even in mild gardens. The gilded sage with a yellow margin mentioned by Rea, which today is called 'Icterina', is the best of all coloured leaf sages for it is compact, hardy, keeps it colour throughout the year and never seems to flower. Today the lesser sage, so prized by herbalists of 400 years ago, is so rare as to be almost unknown. It is difficult to know why a plant once so highly prized is no longer grown, especially with the recent upsurge of interest in growing herbs. All the garden books of the sixteenth and seventeenth centuries described it as tender, yet this is no excuse for its disappearance; there are other tender herbs which are still with us. The lesser sage is *Salvia officinalis minor* which visually seems to be a smaller edition of the common sage in size and height of bush, leaf dimension and length of flower spike; leaves, which are usually greyer, have when crushed a different fragrance, being milder and more musky. In spite of its reputation for tenderness it seems as hardy as the other forms of common sage and is certainly more reliable than Tricolor.

In a garden, common sage needs to be positioned in full sun, in a well drained, not overrich soil, and its fragrance and oil content seem to be enhanced by the application of lime. It is reasonably hardy and will survive all but the coldest winters. Winter wet causes more damage than extreme dry cold and after damp winters, bushes can look bedraggled by spring. Although in mild districts, sage can make large and old bushes, it is best to treat as a short term crop, replanting every three or four years. Propagation is most usually by cuttings taken in late summer of young growth. Root the cuttings in pots or boxes in a very sandy mix to which some soil has been added. Keep the rooted cuttings under glass until the following spring and plant out when the danger of frost is past.

Irrespective of which kind is grown in the garden, the green or the ornamental flowered or foliage forms all can be used in cooking. Fresh material can be taken off bushes at any time of the year and shoots for drying are usually taken off in late summer. Pruning is an essential operation for common sage to keep it tidy and productive and to extend its life. Whereas the removal of shoots for kitchen use can be considered as a form of pruning, it is not enough. Those forms grown for their flowers, and the coloured foliage forms which flower, should be pruned as the flowers fade. Cut the shoots that have bloomed back to where new growth is showing and trim the remaining shoots too so as to shape the bush. The coloured leaf forms which do not flower should be trimmed just before new growth is to begin in the spring. Following pruning, at whatever season, apply a dressing of a general fertiliser lightly over the area of the root spread.

Scarlet Pimpernel

Scarlet pimpernel, the best known name for *Anagallis arvensis*, was immortalised by the Baroness Orczy as a *nom-de-guerre* for Sir Percy Blakeney in her books about the French Revolution. This sprawling plant has long, winged stems with heart-shaped leaves in opposite pairs, from whose axils arise five petalled flowers on short stems. The flowers, which can open and close at predetermined times, will also close when rain is imminent. This ability to foretell time and weather has provided some of the many common names for this plant: 'shepherd's barometer', 'shepherd's warning', 'shepherd's weatherglass', 'shepherd's clock', 'shepherd's dial' and husbandman's warner'. The generic name *anagallis* is derived from a Greek word *anagelae* which means 'to laugh', for an extract was used by the ancients to drive away melancholy; *arvensis* is Latin for a field where scarlet pimpernel can be found as a weed. 'Pimpernel' is of Norman French derivation and refers to the wings of the stems.

Although native throughout much of Europe, including Britain, it is now widespread through most temperate regions of the world as a weed of cultivated land, having arrived as foreign matter amongst cereals and grass seed. While scarlet is the commonest flower colour, blue can be locally common especially in countries of southern Europe, although it is rare in England. At the end of the sixteenth century Gerard said 'I found the female with blew flowers in a chalkie cornfield on the way from Mr William Swanes house at Southfield to Longfield Downs but never anywhere else'. There are many other colours to be found amongst the flowers, for in addition to a range of shades of pink, there are mauves, purples and albinos. In days gone by the red was called the male pimpernel and the blue the female. Legend has it that stock would graze the red but ignore the blue, while in medicine, the male was used to cure ailments among men and the female those among women. From ancient times, scarlet pimpernel had been used in a poultice to draw out thorns, splinters and broken arrow heads that were embedded in the flesh. As its scarlet flower was the colour of blood, it was used to cure by signature not only fresh wounds but also running sores and ulcers. Its use to cure toothache is curious, for a sprig of pimpernel was pushed up the nostril on the opposite side of the face from where the tooth was aching; a cure could also occur if a distillation of pimpernel was poured into the ear on the opposite side of the face from the toothache. The bite of a mad dog was cured by pimpernel, as was the sting of a scorpion or an adder and it also provided protection against the plague, pestilential fever and contagious sickness. An infusion of the blue pimpernel was used by ladies to wash their faces to remove spots, discolouration and rough skin. Legend has it that when planted in a garden it would protect the house from being struck by lightning and the family from spells and incantations by witches and wizards.

Although it is a weed of arable farming, gardens and waste ground, it is never a nuisance and country-folk and town-dwellers alike tolerate it with affection. The size of the flower of the common pimpernel makes it too small to be effective when deliberately planted, but there is a larger red flowered kind known as *phoenicium* sometimes offered in seed catalogues, and a larger blue which can be listed as either *grandiflorum* or *coeruleum*. These superior forms of the scarlet or blue pimpernels can be used in bedding, annual borders or as fillers or ground cover amongst shrubs or herbaceous plants; they look especially effective when sown direct into a narrow border along the side of a path or against a house.

Grow in full sun, in a poor dry soil (preferably with some lime), where they will remain fairly small and flower freely; in shade, in wet or rich soil, there is excessive and lush growth, producing large coarse leaves which hide the sparse flowers. Sow seed in early spring where plants are to flower and thin the seedlings to stand 6in. (150mm) apart; once established, the scarlet pimpernel will self sow, reappearing every year, and it is easy to remove if it wanders from its allotted place or it comes up too thickly.

——— *Scilla Bifolia* ———

It is curious that a plant so long in cultivation is best known today by its botanical name when the English have an aversion for names which are foreign. *Scilla bifolia* is widely distributed from southern Europe to western Asia, usually as a woodland plant. In the seventeenth century it was lumped together with a number of different genera under 'Hyacinth'. These included hyacinth proper, which is best known today as the plant we grow in bowls for winter decoration. The hairy, grape and musk hyacinths were in the genus *Muscari,* while Indian or tuberous hyacinths were the florist's tuberose or *Polianthes tuberosa.* Starry hyacinths, sometimes spelt jacint or iacinth, are what we now classify as species of *Scilla* although in the seventeenth century, *Scilla* was used for *Urginia maritima,* the sea squill or sea onion. *S. bifolia* came into England sometime during the sixteenth century from France and Germany and was called 'starry hyacinth', sometime prefaced by 'French' or 'German', to indicate country of origin, and 'early', to distinguish it from *S. italica* which, flowering much later, was called 'summer' or 'late flowering' starry hyacinth. This early starry hyacinth was grown by all the well known gardeners of the seventeenth century: Gerard, Parkinson, Sir Thomas Hanmer, Rea and Tradescant (father and son). At that period there were many more colours available than there are today: in addition to blue and white there were pink, red, violet, purple and ash-coloured. This plant remained popular until the twentieth century, when it lost favour to the paler blue *Scilla sibirica,* which flowers three or more weeks later.

   Scilla bifolia grows only a few inches above the ground, and although it is usual for there to be only two leaves, as indicated by the specific epithet, it can have three or even four. Its shoots push through the ground as soon as the snow has gone or when there is no snow, from mid to late winter. Almost as soon as the shoot appears, the flower bud is pushing its way into the light to grow almost horizontally, to produce an inflorescence which is triangular in outline, for the oldest flowers are born on short stalks which may be ½in. (13mm) long, while the youngest flowers seem to be stemless. The most common colour is a rich medium blue with just a hint of purple, which is more beautiful than all the colour selections that have been made over the centuries. In any large sweep of these bulbs can be found flowers that are white or occasionally pink. Unless these are selected, removed and kept in isolation they never seem to prosper and soon disappear. One form that appears in bulb catalogues is the botanical variety *praecox* which has greater vigour, is more upright and in most years flowers up to a week earlier than the normal type.

In its native countries, *S. bifolia* forms carpets in deciduous woodland and it will establish and make colonies under trees or amongst shrubs in a garden. It seems to thrive in a cool, moist soil that does not dry out, wherever snowdrops are happy. Unlike snowdrops, though, it is not happy when growing under grass unless the sward is thin. Planting should take place in autumn as soon as the bulbs become available in shops, supermarkets, garden centres or nurseries. Fork over the soil, working in organic matter in the form of peat or leaf mould, and then firm with the feet. Plant the bulbs in groups by pushing each into the soil or using a dibber at 2in. (50mm) spacing, with the tip of the bulb about an inch (25mm) below the surface. Once planted, bulbs should be left undisturbed until they become overcrowded or decline in vigour. When this happens, lift as they go out of flower, pull the clumps to pieces and replant.

Siberian Wallflower

Few flowers are more brilliant than the orange Siberian wallflower yet in recent years it has been neglected even though strong colours such as orange-scarlet and shocking pink have been much sought after. There is some uncertainty as to its origin: it is generally considered to be a cross between what we must now call *Erysimum decumbens* from the Pyrenees and the Caucasian *E. perofskianum* which was raised by a John Marshall in 1846. Two seedlings resulted from this cross, one with yellow flowers and the other orange; to these and their offspring was given the name *Cheiranthus marshallii* or 'Marshall's wallflower'. Doubts have been raised as to whether this is in fact a hybrid, and some botanists consider the Siberian wallflower to be a selection of *E. perofskianum*. There is an interesting comment in the book *Cultivated Plants, their Propagation and Improvement* by F. W. Burbridge, published in 1877: 'I have often tried to get seed from *Cheiranthus Marshallii* but without success . . .'

Several questions come to be asked about the names for this plant. Should it belong in the genus *Cheiranthus* or *Erysimum*? It can appear in seed catalogues under either. When neither of its reputed parents are from eastern Asia, why 'Siberian wallflower'? Why the modern epithet of *allionii*? This suggests that it was raised by Carlo Allionii, a professor at Turin University, but he had died almost 40 years before this plant was introduced.

Taxonomists have shuffled many species between the genera *Cheiranthus* and *Erysimum*. During the last century the species mentioned here were more usually classified in *Cheiranthus*, today in *Flora Europea* both are now with *Erysimum*. Confusion had arisen between *C. marshallii* and *E. marschallianum*, which did originate from Siberia, so a common name came to be wrongly applied. It seems to be Gringan who used the name *allionii* first in *Revue Horticole* in 1912; perhaps he did not accept that

Common Sage, Salvia officinalis

Ten Week Stock

the Siberian wallflower was of hybrid origin.

In spite of its confused history, this is a very attractive biennial for late flowering in spring bedding, although it could be used as a temporary filler for herbaceous border, island bed, rock garden or shrub border; flower stems are too short for use as cut flowers. The yellow Siberian wallflower is easy to use, but the orange needs to be carefully placed otherwise its strong colour can kill or clash with others. In spring bedding it can be used as ground cover with Dutch Iris, of the palest shades of either blue or yellow.

Seed is sown in nursery beds in midsummer in rows 12in. (300mm) apart with the resulting seedlings thinned to stand 6in. (150mm) apart or planted out at the same spacings. These are then transplanted to the places in the garden where they are to flower in early autumn.

Soapwort

'Soapwort' is but one common name indicating the cleansing properties of this plant; others are 'soapweed', 'suds', 'fuller's-wort', 'fuller's-herb', 'fuller's-weed' and 'scourwort', while other names are 'bouncing Bet', 'goodbye-to-summer' and 'bruisewort'. In earlier centuries its sticky sap, which in water would produce a lather, was used for washing the body, clothes, linen, for cleaning tapestries, taking marks out of cloths and for washing treen and pewter. Medicinally it has been used on green wounds, tumours and ulcers and as a poultice applied to bruises and inflammations to ease pain and remove the discoloration from the skin; it was also claimed to be a cure for venereal diseases.

Saponaria officinalis is a native of southern Europe, and although found in many places throughout Britain, it is always close to habitation and often on banks of streams and rivers, where it has naturalised. It is a plant that was much used in earlier times for cleansing wool, and until the present century spinning and weaving mills were built by streams or rivers, for they were water powered. It must have been taken to the New World by the Pilgrim Fathers, and in some of the eastern states it is locally common, but it is usually found on or close to ruins of old textile mills. It is said to have been used by early settlers in the United States as a protection against or to alleviate the pain caused by the poison ivy.

Probably this plant had been brought over to England by the Normans for its cleansing properties, but the double flowered form was taken into gardens during the sixteenth century. For more than 400 years its popularity has waxed and waned, but it has always retained its appeal to cottagers. White is the colour of the flowers of wild plants, and it was the double white which was first taken into gardens. Occasionally one can find wild single pinks or reds, but it is the doubles which are the most appreciated in gardens, the colour deepening as the flowers age.

Soapwort, a plant of a suckering habit, is planted at the front of a herbaceous border or island bed where if left to its own devices it will form an extensive patch. It produces many upright shoots which can reach 2ft (600mm), to carry a profusion of quite large flowers from midsummer until late autumn. When the herbaceous border or island bed is being lifted for replanting, clumps of soapwort can be pulled apart into reasonable sized pieces for replanting. Give each plenty of space 2–3ft (600–1000mm)) and do not overplant, for it can be invasive and swamp choicer neighbours.

Spanish Broom

Spartium junceum, which is widespread in southern Europe and North Africa, makes a medium to large shrub, although with age it can make a small tree which can exceed 15ft (5m). It produces pithy green stems, round in cross-section, which resemble rushes (species of *Juncus,* as indicated in the specific epithet). Although a few small leaves are produced on new growth in spring, these are retained only for a few weeks before being shed, and the green stems perform the functions of leaves. From midsummer until the frosts arrive there is a succession of quite large pea-like yellow flowers to be followed by a cluster of pods which in most years provide ripe seed.

Spartium (Spanish broom), *Spartina* (a genus of grasses of which *S. stricta,* chord grass, is found on British salt marshes) and *esparto* (which refers to *Stipa tenacissima,* a grass from southern Spain used to stabilise sand-dunes), have all been used for making ropes or weaving mats and are all derived from a Greek word *spartion* which indicates this use. *Spartium junceum* was an early entrant to British gardens, for it was already well established in the sixteenth century. In 1548 William Turner, who was physician to the Duke of Somerset, was growing this plant 'in my Lordes gardin at Shene, and in my Lord Cobhams gardin a little fro(m) Graves End'. During this period it was referred to as 'French broom', sometimes 'Greek broom', because of the similarity to the English broom (*Sarothamnus (Cytisus) scoparius*) which was used for making besoms as was the Spanish broom. Because of its use in weaving, another common name was 'weavers' broom', while in the present century it has been called 'yellow sweet pea', a name attributed to E. A. Bowles because of its resemblance to the flowers of that plant when worn in a button-hole.

Dioscorides in '*Materia Medica*' had advocated its use as a purging herb, as did Gerard in his Herbal 'The flowers and seed of Spanish Broom are good to be drunke with Meade or honied water in the quantities of a dram to cause one to vomite with great force and violence. If taken alone, it looseneth the belly, driveth forth great quantitie of waterie and filthie humours'. Parkinson warned against taking it internally as it caused vomiting, but when used externally as a poultice it eased the pain of sciatica.

It was offered for sale in the catalogue of William Lucas in 1677, and in the closing years of the seventeenth century London and Wise, who had a nursery at Brompton, were training Spanish broom into standards which they were using to plant boscage, in which the framework of the tree was trimmed to resemble a hedge on top of the trunks. In the catalogue of William and John Perfect of Pontefract, published in 1777, Spanish Broom plants were offered for sale at three pence each which, allowing for the difference in values, probably corresponds closely to what a gardener would pay for one today. Peter Collinson, a wealthy London draper and a patron of plant collectors, had introduced a double flowered form of the Spanish broom into England in 1746, having paid a golden ducat for a bush in Nuremburg. Following propagation, plants were given to Christopher Gray, who had a nursery at Fulham, and to James Gordon with his nursery at Mile End.

Spanish broom is a useful plant for a shrub border, for it comes into flower after spring flowering shrubs have finished. Plant a pot-grown specimen in a well drained soil, either acid or alkaline, in full sun when the danger of frost has passed and cut hard back to ensure plenty of growth from ground level. Once established, it can be left to its own devices but trim to shape in early spring or cut hard back at this same season if the bush becomes over-large. Seed is the easiest method of propagation of the single flowered form. Sow in gentle heat in early spring after soaking the seed for 24 hours in cold water. The double, which is more of a curiosity than a thing of beauty, can be increased by taking off short side-shoots of non-flowering growth and treating them as cuttings under protection.

Spotted Dead Nettle

This plant is called 'nettle' because of leaf shape and hairiness; 'dead' because the hairs are non-stinging, and 'spotted' because of the white mark on the central portion of the leaf.

Lamium maculatum is widespread in Europe, from northern Germany to the Mediterranean, and now also throughout the temperate regions of North America and Australia, having arrived there as impurities in farm seed. It is an evergreen perennial producing a mat of growth from which arise upright stems up to 8in. (200mm) tall in full light, but in shade they can be twice this length. The stems, which are square in cross-section, have opposite leaves, with each pair at right angles to those above and below.

139

The heart-shaped leaves, about 2in. (50mm) long and almost as wide, have margins with rounded teeth; usually, but not always, there is a white mark or blotch in the central portion of the upper surface which like the lower is covered with short hairs. The cells which make up this mark are filled with air, which is why they appear to be white. In the upper leaf axils during spring clusters of narrow hooded flowers are produced, usually about an inch (25mm) in length and mauvish pink in colour.

The first mention of this plant is in the Greek *Herbal* of Dioscorides, written during the first century AD, a book which was to form the basis of medicine for about 1500 years throughout Europe and into Asia. This book was translated into English by John Goodyer in 1665 and was edited, at least as far as the names were concerned, by John Gunther in 1933. *Lamium maculatum* is almost certainly a Gunther name, for with it is *leukas,* which can be assumed to be Goodyer's anglicisation of the Greek. According to Dioscorides, the plants 'when drunk are good with wine against ye venom of poisonous creatures especially those of the sea'. In the sixteenth and seventeenth centuries there are references to this plant: John Parkinson includes it in *Theatrum Botanicum* of 1640; William Coles has a description which corresponds with this plant in *Adam in Eden* (1657); and it was being grown in Scotland's first botanic garden at Edinburgh in 1673. Casper Bauhin in *Pinax Theatrica Botanici*, published in 1657, says that *Lamium maculatum* is included with *L. album* in Gerard's *Herbal*. In the 1597 edition of this work there is a footnote to *L. album*, white dead nettle, which says, 'there is also a variety of this having red or purple flowers'. Thomas

Johnson, in the 1633 revision, adds more information which leaves no doubt that the plant referred to was *L. maculatum*. It is curious that this plant does not appear in Linnaeus's *Species Plantarum* of 1753 nor in Aiton's *Hortus Kewensis* of 1789 and its later edition. In the first edition of the *British Flora* published in 1858, George Bentham considered it to be no more than a form of *L. album*, so it may be that its uncertain status is why there are so few references to it in books.

In the seventeenth century, it was called together with a number of other species of *Lamium*, 'archangel', a common name today reserved for the yellow flowered plant which has undergone several changes in recent years: *Lamium galeobdolon*, *Galeobdolon luteum* and *Lamiastrum galeobdolon*. In the sixteenth and seventeenth centuries, archangel was used solely in medicine; there is no mention of it being grown for the beauty of its flowers. This is surprising, for even if it was brought into the garden from the countryside, it is just as attractive as many others that did find favour. All the species of *Lamium* which were referred to as archangel had the same virtues: 'archangel bruised with some salt and vinegar or with Hogs lard upon any hard tumours or swelling, and that in the neck or throat which is called Kings Evil (a glandular swelling, perhaps goitre) doth help to dissolve and discusse them in like manner applied to Gout, Sciatica and other Joynte-aches or Sinews doth very much allay the pains and give ease'. 'Likewise it stauncheth the bleeding of the nose and mouth if the Herb be stamped and applied to the nape of the neck'. 'The flowers are baked with sugar as roses are, which is called sugar roset; also the distilled water of them which is used to make the heart merry; to make a good colour in the face and to make the vitall spirits more fresh and lively'. Because there was a similarity between the half moons which appear at the base of fingernails and the spot on the leaf, this plant was thought to cure by signature conditions of the nails. It was considered to provide protection against demons and evil spirits and so was often planted in cottage gardens, and was included in nosegays which in addition to disguising unpleasant smells, protected the carrier from demons and evil spirits and warded off the plague.

After the seventeenth century, it was completely out of favour until the second half of the twentieth century. Its return seems to be associated with the fashion of ground cover plants under trees and shrubs to reduce the need for weeding. Planted fairly close together it quickly forms a close carpet and so prevents weeds from establishing. Under such conditions, to keep it tidy and dense it could be sheared back to ground level after flowering, with new growth quickly forming new carpet.

As with many plants the time of flowering varies, and so does the colour of its flowers and foliage; the best of these colours have been selected and given cultivar names. There are two cvs with identical rose or shell-pink flowers, *Salmoneum* and *Roseum*; the former is more sprawling and the flowers are a little smaller but it is the first to come into bloom, often during the winter; the latter is more upright, has slightly larger flowers but does not come into flower until six weeks after the former. In *album*, the flowers are of a good clean white but the plant is the last of all to flower, at the end of spring. The form *aureum* has a yellow leaf and makes an attractive foliage plant, but it should never be allowed to flower for the purplish mauve colour clashes with the leaf colour. This is a weak grower, especially on a dry soil, and it tends to burn in full sun. Two cultivars Beacon Silver and Chequers, which appeared simultaneously in English gardens about 10 years ago, have leaves which are almost completely silver; both are good plants and similar in appearance. In winter, there is a very narrow green margin on Beacon Silver and its flowers are reddish pink, whereas Chequers has a broader marginal band and flowers are a mauvish pink. The leaves of both in full sun become spotted or blotched with red as flower stems develop which spoils their appearance. If, at this stage, plants are sheared back to ground level, new growth quickly returns with leaves of pristine whiteness. When planted in light shade, however, the staining of the leaves does not occur. Because of the similarity of these two cvs, there is probably not room for both and Beacon Silver seems to be eclipsing Chequers. Another with the same leaf colour is White Nancy, but this has white flowers and it does not produce spotted or blotched leaves at flowering. An interesting curiosity of these white or silver leafed forms is to see them on a cold frosty morning when the leaves appear to have turned green, and yet if a sprig is broken off and taken into a warm room, the whiteness reappears within a few minutes. These selected forms can all be used as ground cover but they have other uses in a garden: for planting at the front of a herbaceous border, island beds, a foliage border or for spring bedding as foliage or flowering plants through which bulbs can grow. A pleasing sight is to see *Tulipa fosteriana*, 'Red Emperor', growing through a carpet of Beacon Silver.

All forms can be easily propagated from cuttings taken of non-flowering growth at any time of the year.

Stock

In *Matthiola incana*, the generic name commemorates the Italian botanist Pierandrea Mattioli, who lived between 1500 and 1577 often quoted by John Gerard in his *Herbal*, while the specific epithet means 'hoary'. It is a perennial plant of cliffs and coastal areas of southern Europe and may be truly wild on the Isle of Wight. It has thick, often woody stems, which become much branched with terminal clusters of grey, hairy spoon- or lance-shaped leaves. The main flower spike develops in late winter to produce white or purplish-mauve fragrant flowers; branches developing from the main stems extend flowering throughout spring and even into early summer.

In classical times this plant together, with wallflower, was referred to as *Leucoion* in Greek and *Viola alba* in Latin, which translates into English as white violet'. It retained the scientific name of *Viola alba* or *Leucoion album* right into the seventeenth century, whilst Linnaeus in 1753 classified it as *Cheiranthus incanus*; by the sixteenth century in English it had become 'stock gilliflower'. Just as in classical times, 'violet' was a general plant name and may have borne no resemblance to the plant we now know as 'violet', so 400 years ago, 'gilliflower' (variously spelt) was used as a common name for many unrelated plants. 'Gilliflower' without an adjective was 'carnation'. One of the oldest scientific names for carnation, sometimes used also as a common name, was *caryophyllus* (now its specific epithet); in French this was *gilofre* and this had become corrupted to gillifleur and translated back into English as 'July Flower'. In addition to 'stock gilliflower', there is 'yellow stock gilliflower' for wallflower, 'bulb-stock gilliflower' for snowdrop or snowflake, and 'sea-stock gilliflower' for *Verbascum spinosum*. In the eighteenth century, Philip Miller was to call it 'hoary stock gilliflower' or 'queen's gilliflower', but throughout the nineteenth century in fact as late as 1911 in England it was called 'stock gilliflower', and one can find this same word used in North America for another 18 years. The word 'stock' is meant to indicate 'woody' as in 'rootstock' and, 'stock' came to be used as an alternative to 'stock gilliflower' from the time of the First World War onwards.

The stock was probably brought into England at the time of the Norman Conquest, and it was well established in English gardens by the sixteenth century. William Turner grew a single white and a purple in 1548, and by 1597 Gerard had added pink to the list as well as flowers that were striped. In the 1633 revision of Gerard's *Herbal*, Thomas Johnson mentions double flowers and says that many of these were grown in the garden of Mr Ralph Tuggie. In 1629, Parkinson had the single yellow and mentioned a double of the same colour but said it was a stranger to this country. Sir Thomas Hanmer had, amongst singles, deep violet, bright light crimson, pure white and cream; and amongst doubles, purple or tawny and some striped with white. He wrote, 'They write of a double yellow but tis a stranger yet in England'. John Rea, however, in 1665 was saying, 'The double yellow stock gilliflower is as rare to find as a white wallflower yet there are of both sorts double as well as single'.

Towards the end of the seventeenth century an unbranched type with deep pink or red flowers was introduced by the nurserymen, London and Wise, which came to be called Brompton Stock after their nursery.

Throughout the eighteenth century, stock continued to be widely grown in the gardens of the gentry for its fragrance, but it was only the doubles which were tolerated. It had long been realised that the doubles were sterile but that plants raised from seed collected from garden-bred singles would produce a large percentage of doubles. Almost all books written during the eighteenth century make recommendations, often contradictory, for the cultivation of single flowered kinds. These were banished to the kitchen garden, where they were allowed to seed in the hope of producing an ever higher percentage of doubles. Stock seed, if sown early in the year, would provide some flowers by the autumn when it was possible to rogue out the singles. Stock was considered to be tender, and throughout the seventeenth and eighteenth centuries recommendations were made to transplant seedlings in poor ground, even suggesting the incorporation of sand to achieve this (a plant growing in a barren soil grew slowly and hard and was more cold resistant than a lush plant in rich soil). In the eighteenth century, plants were often kept throughout the winter under glass in large containers in which they were allowed to flower under cover, although these pots could be transferred to the garden in spring as temperatures rose. In the following century protected crops provided cut flowers for sale by florists, for the fragrant flowers were much in demand. When spring bedding became fashionable towards the end of the century, stocks were used in milder gardens for spring display, often being kept under glass until the coldest part of the winter was over before planting out.

A hardier strain was raised during the nineteenth century known as East Lothian stocks, which had resulted from crossing *M. incana* with *M. sinuata*. This strain extended the season of the ordinary stock, for the gardener could have some in flower over much of the year by making periodic sowings. Those sown in summer could be used outside in spring bedding if transplanted in early autumn. Late winter sowings under glass or early spring sowings outside would provide plants for summer bedding or for cut flowers.

While *M. incana* is a perennial and flowers outside from late winter until early summer, there is a botanical variety, *M. incana var annua*, which is a true annual and has been used for summer bedding display. This is the plant we know as 'ten-week stock' because that is said to be the period it takes from sowing to flowering. It was introduced into England at the beginning of the eighteenth century and appears in Miller's *Gardener's Dictionary* as *Cheiranthus annuus*, which he called the 'lesser stock gilliflower' or 'ten-week stock'. He had red, purple, pink, and white, both singles and doubles. As in *M. incana* the doubles are sterile and it is from plants with single flowers that seed is obtained to produce the doubles. In 1951, the Danish seed firm of Hansen introduced a strain in which the seed leaves of plants which were going to produce double flowers were of a paler colour than the singles, and so it became possible to rogue at the pricking-out stage.

Stocks are reliable outside only in mild gardens where winters are not severe, but they can be pot-grown for cold glasshouse display. Seed is sown, outside in midsummer in a nursery bed where the soil is rather poor. When large enough, either thin the seedlings to stand 4–6in- (100–150mm) apart or transplant to the same distance. The soil in the beds into which the plants will be finally transplanted should have no organic matter incorporated, but should be given a dressing of potash and phosphate with some lime; these beds should be in a warm part of the garden sheltered from cold winds. During the growing season, following transplanting from the seed bed, and in early spring, spray at frequent intervals to control aphis, for this pest is responsible for the transfer of a virus disease which causes flower colour to break. East Lothian stocks can be sown at intervals throughout the year either outside or under glass depending on when they are wanted in flower. Sowing of ten-week stock should be made at intervals to extend flowering. The first can be made under glass in early spring for planting into flower beds in early summer; later sowings outside will provide flowers for cutting.

Sunflower

The botanical name for sunflower is *Helianthus annuus,* with the specific epithet describing the length of its life. Helianthus is Latin for 'the sun' and common names, irrespective of language, have the same or a similar meaning because of the form of the flower. Other English names are 'flower-of-the-sun', 'golden flower of Peru', 'greatest Indian sunflower', whilst in North America it is gold(s) gloden, and lareablell.

Helianthus annuus is native to the southern United States, where it makes a much branched plant with many flower heads often no more than 4in. (100mm) in diameter. It must have been taken into South America in ancient times, for in Peru it was to become a staple crop to provide oil, and it played a part in Inca religious ceremonies. It was these highly cultivated plants with single large flowers that were taken into Europe by the Spanish conquerors when they returned home. The first mention of the plant in English seems to be in a book of 1577 by John Frampton, *Joyfull News out of the Newfounde Worlde* which was a translation of a work by Doctor Monardes, a botanist of Seville, which had been published in Spain over a period of five years between 1569 and 1574. John Gerard was growing it in his garden at Holborn in 1596 and it was illustrated in his *Herbal* published in the following year. Whilst this may have been the first illustration to be seen in England, the woodcuts which were used in the *Herbal* had been obtained by the publisher, John Norton, from Frankfurt where they had been used in 1590 in *Eicones Plantarum* by Tabermontanus. In 1607 the sunflower was being grown by Sir John Salusbury at Lleweny; in 1629, by

John Parkinson at Ludgate Hill, and by William Cleybrooke at Nash Court in Kent in 1632. If one is to believe John Rea, by 1665 its popularity was waning: 'heretofore admired but now grown common, not at all respected'. In spite of John Rea, it remained fashionable in English gardens throughout the next three centuries.

According to Gerard the immature flower buds were eaten in the same way as those of globe artichoke: 'the buds before they be floured, boiled and eaten with butter, vinegar and pepper after the manner of the artichoke are exceedingly pleasant meate, surpassing the Artichoke far in procuring bodily lust'. Although the Incas had grown sunflowers for the oil obtained from their seed, it was not to become an important crop plant in warmer countries of the world until the twentieth century. Today a dwarf strain less than 12in (300mm) high has been bred which will allow mechanical harvesting. Philip Miller wrote that the seed was used for feeding poultry, and it has continued to be grown for this purpose. Another animal use is as oil cake, prepared from the seed remains after oil extraction, which is used to feed cattle. Seeds have been and still are in some countries eaten as a nut, for the kernel has a taste reminiscent of almonds. It is claimed that the pith from the stems is the lightest vegetable substance known and it has been used in the manufacture of life-saving devices at sea.

As a garden plant today the sunflower remains more of a curiosity than a thing of beauty. It is one of the garden plants favoured by children in their first garden, for the rate of growth is so rapid that they can imagine they can see the plant growing. In competitions organised by schools for children and by gardening clubs for adults, there are fequently prizes for the person who can grow the tallest sunflower. As long ago as 1597, John Gerard was saying that a plant in his garden had reached 14ft (4.3m) and had a flower 16in. (400mm) in diameter, and both he and Crispin van de Passe refer to one in the Royal Garden in Madrid which reached 24ft (6m) (one wonders how plants of these heights were able to support themselves).

For the flower garden a smaller race of sunflowers have been bred which rarely exceed 6ft (2m), with branched stems and smaller flowers which more closely resemble the wild type. Most are yellow, single or double, there is one with variegated foliage and there are some real dwarfs at no more than 3ft (1m) in height. There are also some with red or reddish flowers: seed collected by a Mrs Cockerell from a red-flowered plant she had found growing by the roadside near Boulder in Colorado in 1910 produced the parents from which this strain was bred.

The sunflower is an annual and has large seeds. These can be sown individually where they are to flower by pushing two seeds into the ground; if both germinate, one can be removed. Allow plenty of space when sowing in a group because of the height that each can reach. The earliest sowing outside in late spring will be in flower by the end of summer or in early autumn. For earlier flowering and when competing for the tallest stem, sow seed in gentle heat under glass in early spring and plant out when their is no longer any frost. Groups of the large-flowered sunflower can be grown at the back of a shrub border, whilst the smaller flowered type can be grouped in a herbaceous border or island bed, and the real dwarfs can be used in bedding.

Virginia Stock

It has never been explained why 'Virginia' has been applied to this plant, it has no connection with North America, for it originated in southern Europe. Some of the earliest names applied to the plant, which was introduced into England in 1713, were: 'lesser dames violet', 'small dames violet', 'maritime dames violet', all of which compare it with *Hesperis matrionalis* which is called dames violet. In addition there is also 'dwarf stock gilliflower' and 'dwarf annual stock gilliflower', in which it is associated with a stock. Philip Miller, in the 1738 edition of his *Gardener's Dictionary* had used 'Virginia stock gilliflower', and the Reverend William Hanbury in *A Complete Body of Plant and Gardening* had referred to it as 'dwarf Virginian Stock July Flower'. Within 30 years of its introduction, 'Virginia' had been attached to it and there was one Mrs Loudon who attempted to explain it, by suggesting that it should have been called 'virgin's stock' because of its easiness of culture, rendering it fit for the care of young girls. It had been classified with the wallflowers by Linnaeus who had called it *Cheiranthus maritimus,* but was reclassified by Robert Brown who called it *Malcolmia maritima,* in which the generic name commemorates a nurseryman. Three generations of nurserymen of a family called Malcolm had owned nurseries at Kennington, Stockwell and Kensington between 1788 and 1835, and it seems that Robert Brown's name commemorated one of two Williams who were father and son in the first and second generations. It has proved to be a consistently popular plant because it is so easy to grow and takes only a few weeks to come into flower; it has always been one of the packets of seed given to children for their first gardens.

It can be used in an annual border, to line a path, for extremely narrow borders and as a filler on the rock garden, for the front of a herbaceous border or an annual border and amongst shrubs. Seed can be scattered over the ground and raked in, but the resulting seedlings become mixed with annual weeds and these are difficult to control. It is preferable to take out shallow drills 4–6in. (100–150mm) apart and sow the seed very thinly, thinning the resulting seedlings to stand 4in. (100mm) apart. Make the first sowing in early spring and continue at two weekly intervals throughout the summer so as to provide a succession of flowers. If the sowing is continued into the autumn, these late seedings will overwinter and begin to flower early in the following spring.

Wallflower

Whether by their bright colours or their nostalgic fragrance, wallflowers have held gardeners' affection for at least 400 years. 'Wallflower' is an appropriate name for this plant that is so often found on walls of ruined buildings. In the language of flowers, it has become the emblem of fidelity through misfortune; for the desolate, it enlivens the ruins of time that neglect would otherwise cause.

Cheiranthus cheri occurs in southern Europe and extends into western Asia, although it is often common outside its natural range due to escapes from cultivation. Both the generic name and the specific epithet are derived from the Arabic word *keri* and this same word and 'cheri' were both used as old English common names. In classical times, herbalists classified the wallflower with the stock, as *Leucoion* in Greek or *Viola alba* in Latin, which in English became 'white violet'. In the late Middle Ages, violet was a general plant name and the flowers to which it referred may have no resemblance to the flower which we know by that name today. *Leucoion* and *Viola* were retained up to the seventeenth century with the specific epithet *Viola alba* for stock and *Viola lutea* for wallflower. Although 'yellow violet' was sometimes used for wallflower, it was more often called 'yellow-stock gilliflower' although 'wallstock gilliflower' and 'winter stock gilliflower', even 'winter July-flower', were other alternatives. For red wallflowers there were other names: 'bleeding heart', 'blood drops of Christ', 'bleeding fingers', 'bloody fingers', and 'bloody warrior', the latter, in addition to being used as a common name, became a cv name for a double flowered red.

The wallflower seems to have been introduced into England at the time of the Norman Conquest, probably accidentally when the Normans were bringing in stone from Normandy to build castles. Already by the end of the thirteenth century, the wallflower is recorded as growing on derelict castles. William Turner in 1548 said, 'One is called in English Cheiry, Hertes-ease or wal gelefloure, it groweth upon walles and in the springe of the yere, it hath yellow flowers'. By the end of the century Gerard was growing in his garden at Holborn a large-flowered yellow which he describes as having flowers as big as a sovereign; he was also growing a double yellow. Some 30 years later John Parkinson, in addition, was growing a single pale yellow, a red and a white as well as a double red. Sir

Thomas Hanmer and John Rea both grew a double white which Sir Thomas describes as rare and tender.

All the plants in a garden in the seventeenth century had to be useful, even if they had beautiful or fragrant flowers. An oil prepared from the flowers was used in toiletry. Flowers and leaves provided an infusion to cure apoplexy, palsy, gout, sores and ulcers of the mouth. In Gerard's *Herbal* we can read: 'The leaves stamped with a little bay salt, and bound round the wrists of the hand take away the shaking fits of the ague'.

Doubleness in flowers arises either from an increase in the number of petals or when the stamens and/or stigma become petaloid. When stamens and stigma are present, seed will be produced, but when they are missing because they have changed their form, the flower will be sterile. In the eighteenth century, Philip Miller called any wallflower 'double' where the bloom had more than four petals, but he also described the other kind of doubleness, saying that the former could be raised from seed but that the latter was increased by cuttings. Doubles which could be raised from seed continued to be grown throughout the nineteenth century and were still available in the early years of the twentieth at least in Germany; it is doubtful if any seedsman lists them today. Of the full doubles that are raised from cuttings, the best known is Harpur-Crewe, which was named for the Reverend Harpur-Crewe, a nineteenth-century cleric. This wallflower bears a close resemblance to a double yellow known to Parkinson; indeed, it seems to be the same plant. Throughout the centuries it has happened not infrequently that old plants have been reintroduced under new names, sometimes to deceive but more often because an earlier name was unknown or had been forgotten. Another very old double is the red Bloody Warrior, and there is a double pale yellow called Miss Jekyll. None of these full doubles have great vigour, probably because they are infected with a debilitating virus disease which has no symptoms but means that the affected plants are short-lived and difficult to propagate.

Plants of Bloody Warrior which have been cleaned of virus grow more strongly and are much easier to propagate from cuttings.

Wallflowers have retained their popularity as garden plants for four hundred years during which they have been treated as perennial plants. After their spring display was over they were trimmed with shears, which resulted in a second display in autumn, continuing into the winter. They were considered more as plants for cottage gardens although John Rea, who was a colossal snob, felt that they could be grown in gardens of the gentry: 'Wall-flowers or Winter Gilliflowers have divers sorts worthy of entertainment and although there are some kinds common in every countrey Garden, yet these that follow will deserve a place in this collection, and room in a Florists Garden'. They climbed the social ladder in the second half of the nineteenth century when bedding became a garden fashion. Originally this was intended to provide summer colour at a time when gardens were most in use. Plants that had been used for summer display were removed in autumn before frosts arrived and their place was taken with spring bedding, which consisted of bulbs growing through a ground cover supporting the flower stems of the bulbs and protecting their blooms from mud splashes. Wallflower came to be much used as a ground cover, and seed houses began breeding to extend the colour range from white through all the shades of yellow from cream to orange, and from palest pink to scarlet, crimson, maroon and on to purple. At present there is a much narrower range of colours with dwarfer and more compact plants being the aim of modern day breeding.

While spring bedding is the main way of using these plants, they can also be planted as fillers in a herbaceous border or island bed in bays at the front a shrub border and they may be grown for cut flowers. Seed is sown in summer in nursery beds in rows 12in. (300mm) apart. When large enough seedlings should be thinned to stand 6in. (150mm) apart or lined out to the same distance. This late sowing will produce small plants for transplanting into flower beds but these will establish more easily, be less likely to suffer from wind rock and better able to withstand winter cold than plants with large tops. As soon as the weather warms up in early spring, they will grow away and flower well. There is an aphis-transmitted virus disease which causes colour breaking in the flowers. Spray at regular intervals whenever the weather allows in the seed beds, nursery and flower beds with an aphicide. The doubles will have to be propagated by cuttings which are taken in summer of new growth as it is beginning to mature. Plants are never long lived and have the tendency to suddenly collapse for no apparent reason, so some cuttings should be struck every year. Cuttings, once rooted, should be potted singly and kept under protection over the winter, removing any precocious flowers which may appear and planting out as soon as the danger of frost has past.

Winter Jasmine

With the beginning of the Industrial Revolution, England began to change from a predominantly rural economy to become one of the most highly industrialised nations in Europe. There was a movement of population from villages to towns and cities which increased rapidly in size to accommodate these immigrants. The developing industry began to pollute the atmosphere, which adversely affected plants growing in gardens. The successful garden plants, therefore, were those that could tolerate this pollution and grow satisfactorily in often unsuitable soil where much light was excluded by high privet hedges.

English gardens are spring gardens which reach a peak in May. Plants which extend this season are welcome and while those which provide spectacle in the warm summer months are not difficult to find, a gardener is more restricted when it comes to plants which will be colourful in the coldest months of the year. *Jasminum nudiflorum* is a plant which is winter blooming and able to provide a floral display in the most inhospitable of city gardens. Its popularity has continued to grow since it first came into English gardens in the middle of the nineteenth century, and today it is by far the most common jasmine grown in not only English but also in European gardens, so it could be more properly called 'common jasmine' which is the name retained for *Jasminum officinale*.

J. nudiflorum was discovered growing in gardens around Shanghai by Robert Fortune who brought back plants to England in 1846. Fortune, who was a Scot, moved to England as a young man and at the age of 31 was working with tropical plants in the Horticultural Society's gardens at Chiswick. Following the treaty of Nanking when China was opened up to Europeans, Fortune was sent there to collect plants (although he was to make three trips to China between 1843 and 1862, only the first was sponsored by the Horticultural Society). When the winter jasmine arrived at Chiswick it was grown in a glasshouse until its hardiness was proved, and ever since it has been a popular garden plant.

The winter jasmine is a sprawling shrub rather than a climber like so many other jasmines. It produces long flexuose green angled stems which flop or sprawl over rocks or other shrubs, and will only go up a wall if it is tied to wires or a trellis. It seems to be indifferent to soil. When planted against a wall, it should be remembered that the soil in such a place receives little direct rain and can be very dry; young plants put out in such a position should be well watered until established. Instead of planting at the foot of a wall it can be positioned close to or under a deciduous shrub which can offer support to the thin stems and where the flowers will provide a display before the supporting shrub comes into leaf. If planted against a wall or fence, these should be provided with parallel horizontal wires or a trellis to which stems can be tied. Plant container grown plants in early spring. Following planting, train in a well spaced framework which is secured to a support; check ties annually to ensure that stems are not strangled by string which is too tight. Flowers are produced on previous season's growth, so after the flowers have faded and before new growth begins, all growth which has produced blooms should be cut back to within two or three buds of the framework. This will encourage the production of long stems which will have more and larger flowers during the winter; tie loosely to the wires or trellis as they develop. Cuttings taken in late summer of new growth are easy to root in a frame or a glasshouse. For those people without such protection some success can be achieved by using hardwood cuttings 6–10in. (150–250mm) long, prepared after the leaves have fallen and inserted to half their length in the open garden. Untied stems which come in contact with the ground will often root and so these layers, when detached and carefully lifted, will produce new plants.

J. nudiflorum 'Aureum' has leaves which are blotched with yellow, and the variegated foliage will provide interest during the summer.

Wood Anemone

'Anemone' is derived from a Greek word which means 'wind'. The earliest kinds of anemone grown in gardens were amongst the harbingers of spring, often blooming on cold winter days. Garden authors of olden times called them 'windflowers' and wrote that they opened only when the wind was blowing. The 'flaw', in 'flawflower', another common name, is a dialect word for 'wind'. It is one of a number of plants to which the name herb-trinity has been given because of the three leaves beneath the flower, and another with religious connotations is 'Our Lady's petticoat'. The wood anemone is a fairy flower, for these wee folk are said to be responsible for painting the lines on the outside of the petals; as night approaches or rain is imminent, the petals fold inwards to form a tent in which fairies sleep or shelter.

Anemone nemorosa extends across northern Europe into Asia, continuing on into North America and coming into Britain. Although it can be found here is hedgerows, it is a plant of the woodland floor forming delightful white carpets in early spring. There are curious branched twig-like rhizomes just below the soil surface which come into growth on mild winter days, but the presence of these anemones is often not noticed until they are about to flowers. The three deeply divided leaves toward the tip of the stem enclose a flower of up to seven petals which while closed display a white underside, veined with any one of a number of colours. The upper surface of the petals, which show themselves on fine dry days, is usually

Ten Week Stock, Matthiola incana annua

Virginia Stock, Malcomia maritima

Wallflower, orange bedder

Mixed Wallflowers

white but it is possible to find the occasional plant showing shadings of pink, mauve or blue in varying depths of colour.

An early immigrant to our gardens, the wood anemone's popularity has waxed and waned over the centuries, always being overshadowed by larger and more brilliant exotic species. Gerard and Parkinson grew a number of coloured forms of wood anemone, both singles and doubles, at the beginning of the seventeenth century but none of the other famous gardeners of the century seem to have grown them; it was however, in the first English botanic garden at Oxford by 1648. It remained out of favour throughout the eighteenth and much of the nineteenth centuries until its cause was taken up by William Robinson. This indefatiguable garden writer brought it to the notice of a wider range of discriminating gardeners along with other neglected plants that had for so long languished in cottage gardens. It was the second half of the nineteenth century which saw the birth of the rock garden fashion that was to develop into a new craze. Robinson was one of the earliest writers for this new style, but its arch-priest was Reginald Farrer. The wood anemone gained Farrer's approval, for in *The English Rock Garden* he wrote 'Though only the common Wood-anemone, need not be ashamed to uphold its seemingly delicate head amongst the proudest beauties of the race'. In the years following the Second World War it was once more out of favour but today its popularity is again in the ascendant. These charming tiny flowers, whether white, pink, mauve or blue, single or double, are delightful in early spring and enthusiasts are searching through nurseries and old gardens hoping to find kinds which they do not have in their own gardens.

Wood anemones seem to be indifferent to soil as long as it is not waterlogged, and is enriched with organic matter in the form of leaf mould. The ordinary single white is probably at its best in a woodland garden where the canopy is not dense. Whilst best in bare soil, it will grow quite well where the ground cover is thin but rarely survives in a thick sward. In the smaller garden, groups of selected forms can be planted amongst shrubs or in pockets on a rock garden. At Kew the ordinary wood anemone has established itself in island beds in the Duke's garden, where the tubers have invaded the crowns of herbaceous plants and even though these are lifted and divided every three years, some tubers always escape the sharp eyes of the gardeners. They quickly recolonise the beds, and provide early patches of colour; by the time the herbaceous plants have come into growth and the earliest are in flower, the wood anemone has died down to its underground rhizome.

Replanting of wood anemones in one's own garden is best done as they pass out of flower and while they can still be easily located; always plant them in groups. When buying, try to obtain container grown plants which will establish more easily. Some bulb firms and garden centres offer dried tubers; these need more attention. When you get them, make up a box with a compost of equal parts of peat and sand and push the tubers into this mixture until they are just covered. As long as the compost is moist at planting time no further watering will be necessary. Keep the boxes in a cool and shady part of the garden and protect from rain; give water only to prevent excessive dryness of the compost. Plant into the garden when the tubers are well rooted or on a mild winter's day as growth begins to push through the soil.

Wormwood

Artemisia absinthium although widespread in Europe, including Britain, is possibly native only to a relatively small region, probably in southern Italy. It has been so long in cultivation, that its appearance elsewhere results from garden escapes. It is a perennial whose tops may die back completely, although it is more usual for it to survive the winter as short perennial shoots. As temperature rise in spring, the shoots develop; on these are alternately arranged leaves which are twice compound with the resulting leaflets divided into three or four lobes. These are dull green above and silver, grey or white beneath. The stems lengthen to produce a terminal inflorescence in the form of a panicle, sometimes compound, of nodding green or grey flowers which become brown as they mature; following pollination and fertilisation fluffy seeds result. This is a vigorous plant and at maturity can be more than 3ft (1m) tall. Plants are variable in shape, height, leaf size and colour. One selection, made by Margery Fish, is called after that lady's house: Lambrooke Silver. This is a spreading plant which does not often exceed 2ft (600mm) but in which the leaves are silvery on both sides. Whereas most forms of *A. absinthum* are truly herbaceous, this is woody, making a low spreading sub-shrub. Most forms of wormwood can be easily increased by taking cuttings at almost any time of the year, but especially in late summer; with Lambrooke Silver however, success seems to come only with spring cuttings.

Artemisia commemorates the Greek goddess Artemis, while *absinthum* is an old Latin word used for the plant. Astrologers considered wormwood to be the herb of Mars; dreams about wormwood were considered to be good omens and brought forth happiness and domestic bliss. In Christian celebrations it is a herb associated, along with species of *Hypericum*, with St John, and girdles of wormwood were worn on his day, 24th June.

For several hundred years this plant has been known as 'wormwood', sometimes 'wormseed'; some writers have included it with other species of *Artemisia* under the name 'southernwood' although this now usually refers to *A. abrotanum*. The Greek *Herbal* of Dioscorides has a name 'apsinthion' which appears to refer to two species: the common wormwood (*A. absinthum*) and the Roman (*A. pontica*). In translation we can read, 'apsinthion hath a warming, binding, digestive facultie and taketh away ye cholerick matter sticking to ye stomach and belly. It is good also for inflamations and ye paines of the belly and ye stomach being drunk with Seseli . . . but with wine for ye poison of Hemlock and Ixia (*Carlina vulgaris*) and ye biting of ye shrew mouse and dragon of the sea'. There is mention in this herbal of a wine called 'absinte' which was made from the Roman absinthe.

Herbalists of the sixteenth and seventeenth centuries list all the cures of Dioscorides and include others as well: when taken before a feast it prevented sickness from overeating, and yet it stimulated a jaded appetite. If a lotion was used to bathe the eyes, it improved vision, took away tiredness and restored their sparkle. It was considered good for the spleen and purified the blood. Some other afflictions for which it was a remedy were: worms, earache and toothache, bad breath, poisoning by toadstools, jaundice, dropsy, quinsy and leprosy. From the very earliest times it had been used for warding off moths from cloths stored in chests. At a time when little attention was paid to hygiene, sprigs of wormwood were steeped in water that was used to wash the body to kill lice, and were added to the straw used to stuff mattresses so as to kill fleas. It is not unknown for leaves to be stripped off plants in spring by birds, who may take them to line their nests to ward off fleas. Alice Coats in her book *Flowers and their Histories*, refers to a 'salve to be made for one suffering from nocturnal goblin visitors'.

Dioscorides had referred to a wine called 'apsinthe', yet reference books suggest that absinthe, much drunk in France, was not introduced until the end of the eighteenth century by one Pernod. When absinthe as a drink was banned because of its harmful properties its place was taken by the drink which came to be called after the introducer of the more harmful one. Today wormwood is one of the ingredients of Vermouth.

In a garden, wormwood is most often to be found in the herb garden. Once introduced, it will self sow and unless rigidly controlled can become a real nuisance. One of the selections such as Lambrooke Silver can be used as a grey border, herbaceous border or island bed or in a group at the front of a shrub border. Whereas the straight species can be easily raised from seed, the selected forms will need to be propagated by cuttings.

BIBLIOGRAPHY

William Aiton-Hortus Kewenis	1789 & 1811
Caspar Bauhin-Pinax Theatri Botanici	1657
W. J. Bean – Trees and Shrubs Hardy in the British Isles	
(8th edition)	1970–1980
Bentham & Hooker (7th edition) British Flora	1947
Thomas Blaikie – Diary of a Scotch Gardener	1931
Bobart – Catalogus Plantarum Hortus Botanici Oxoniensis	1648
F. W. Burbridge – The Propagation & Improvement of	
Cultivated Plants	1877
F. Chittenden – The RHS Dictionary of Gardening	1956
Clapham, Tutin & Warburg – Flora of the British Isles	1962
Alice Coats – Flowers & their Histories	1956
Garden Shrubs & their Histories	1963
The Plant Hunters	1969
William Coles – Adam in Eden	1657
Nicholas Culpepper – The English Physitian	1652
Curtis Botanical Magazine	1787–198?
William Dallimore – Holly, Yew & Box	1908
Alphonse de Candolle – Cultivated Plants & their Improvement	1882
Dioscorides – De Materia Medica edited by R. Gunther	1934
J. Donne – Hortus Cantabrigensis	1823
Elwes & Henry – The Trees of Great Britain & Ireland	1906
John Evelyn – Acetaria	1699
Diary	1819
Directions for the Gardener at Sayes Court edited	
B. Keynes	1932
Kalandarum Hortensis	1664
Sylva	1664
The Compleat Gardiner	1693
Thomas Fairchild – The City Gardener	1722
John J. Finan – Maize in the Great Herbals	1950
Reginald Farrer – The English Rock Garden	1919
Flora Europea	1964–1980
Richard Folkard – Plant Lore, Legends & Lyrics	1884
Robert Fortune – Two Visits to the Tea Districts of China	1853
John Frampton – Joyfull News out of the Newfounde World	1577
H. Friend – Flowers & Flower Lore	1884
John Gardiner – Feate of Gardening	1440
Francois Gentil – Solitary Gardner	1706
John Gerard – Catalogues	1596–1599
Herball	1597–1633

Leo Grindon – Garden Botany   1864
     Shakspere Flors   1883
G.R.T. Gunther – Early English Botanists & their Gardens   1922
William Hanbury – The Complete Body of Planting & Gardening   1770
Thomas Hanmer – The Garden Book – 1659   1933
John Harvey – Early Garden Catalogues   1972
     Early Nurserymen   1974
Blanche Henrey – English Botanical & Horticultural Literature
     before 1800   1975
John Hudson – Florists Companion   1794
Thomas Johnson – Botanical Journeys of 1629 & 1632 edited by
     J. Gilmore   1972
James Justice – The Scots Gardeners Directory   1754
Batty Langley – New Principle of Gardening   1728
Anne Leighton – Early English Gardens in New England   1970
Louis Liger – Compleat Florist   1706
Linnaeus – Species Plantarum   1753
London & Wise – Compleat Gardner (7th edition)   1719
John Loudon – Encyclopaedia of Plants   1829
Jane Loudon – The Ladies Flower Garden   1840
James Maddock – The Florist Directory   1792
Brian Mathew – Dwarf Bulbs   1973
     The Crocus   1982
     Bulbous Plants in Turkey   1984
Mawe & Abercrombie – The Universal Gardener & Botanist
     (2nd edition)   1797
Philip Miller – Gardeners Dictionary   1731 & 1768
John Parkinson – Paradisi in Sole   1629
     Theatrum Botanicum   1640
Joseph Paxton – Botanical Magazine   1843
     Botanical Directory   1868
John Pechey – The Compleat Herbal   1694
Henry Phillips – Flora Historica   1829
Pliny – Historie of the World, 1st century A D   1601
John Rea, Flora, Pomona – Ceres   1676
William Robinson – Alpine Flowers for English Gardens   1870
     Flora & Sylva   1903–1905
Esther Singleton – The Shakespeare Garden   1922
A. E. Speer – Annual & Biennial Plants   1911
William Stearn – A Gardeners Dictionary of Plant Names   1971
Frederick Stern – Snowdrops & Snowflakes   1956
Walahfrid Strabo – Hortulus, 9th century A D   1966
James Sutherland – Hortus Medicus Edinburgensis   1683
William Sutherland – Hardy Herbaceous & Alpine Plants   1871

INDEX

166